OUR AMERICAN HOLIDAYS

MOTHERS' DAY

OUR AMERICAN HOLIDAYS

MOTHERS' DAY

Its History, Origin, Celebration, Spirit,
and Significance as related in
Prose and Verse

COMPILED BY
SUSAN TRACY RICE

EDITED BY
ROBERT HAVEN SCHAUFFLER

GRANGER BOOK CO., INC.
Great Neck, N.Y.

First published 1915
Reprinted 1977

Library of Congress Catalog Number 77-20403

International Standard Book Number 0-89609-075-2

PRINTED IN THE UNITED STATES OF AMERICA

A TRIBUTE TO ALL MOTHERS BECAUSE
OF MY OWN WHOSE ALL EMBRACING
LOVE REACHED OUT TO THE HOMELESS
AND UNPROTECTED OF THE WORLD —
ANIMALS AS WELL AS THE CHILDREN
OF MEN.

S. T. R.

Worthington, Mass.

INTRODUCTION

The arrival of this newcomer, Mothers' Day, in the calendar of our national festivals is significant. That a day so rich in sentiment, so tender in its meaning, should be officially adopted in a country which scoffs at sentiment and prides itself on its veneer of practicality is a hopeful sign. Like the divining rod of old usage it reveals underneath the crust of commercialism a perennial spring of idealism.

Although the formal designation of a specific day as Mothers' Day was but recently made in this country, we find in turning the pages of history that the idea rests, like so many of our customs, upon an ancient foundation. It strikes deep roots into universal truth and emotion. Mother-love antedates the Christian religion. Mother-worship, with its own rites and ceremonies, reaches back into pagan times.

Our earliest record of formal mother-worship is in the stories of the ceremonies by which Cybele, or Rhea, "The Great Mother of the Gods," was worshiped in Asia Minor. In her worship it was the power and majesty of motherhood rather than its tender maternal spirit that the wild dances and wilder music celebrated. Cybele was represented as traversing the mountains in a chariot drawn by lions. The lion, the oak and the pine were sacred to her.

The worship of this superlative " Mother of Gods "

was introduced through Greece into Rome about two hundred and fifty years before Christ. There, it was known as the festival of Hilaria and was held on the Ides of March when the people made offerings in the temple. These were, of course, confiscated by the priests but they served their purpose of elevating motherhood into something of its rightful dignity.

With the advent of Christianity, the festival, still keeping some of its old forms, was informed with a new spirit and transfigured. The old celebration with pagan rites in honor of the " Mother of the Gods " on the Ides of March, grew into a celebration in honor of the " Mother Church." It became the custom on Mid-Lent Sunday, the fourth Sunday in Lent, for the faithful to visit the church in which they were baptized and brought up,— bearing gifts for the altar.

Just when and how this festival of worship for the " Mother Church " gave rise to the observance of " Mothering Sunday " is uncertain. It is sure, however, that a long time ago when young men and maidens were bound out as apprentices and servants, Mid-Lent Sunday was set apart for them to visit their parents. The following quaint account of this festival is taken from Chamber's Book of Days :

" The harshness and general painfulness of life in old times must have been much relieved by certain simple and affectionate customs which modern people have learned to dispense with. Amongst these was a practice of going to see parents, and especially the female one, on the mid Sunday of Lent, taking for them some little present, such as a cake or a trinket. A youth engaged in this amiable act of duty was said to go *a-mothering,* and thence the day itself came to be called Mothering Sunday. One can readily imagine how, after a stripling or maiden had gone to service, or launched in independent housekeeping, the old bonds of filial love would be brightened by this pleasant annual visit, signalized, as custom demanded it should be, by the excitement attending some novel and perhaps surprising gift. There was also a cheering and peculiar festivity appropriate to the day, the prominent dish being *furmety* — which we have to interpret as wheat grains boiled in sweet milk, sugared and spiced. In the northern part of England, and in Scotland, there seems to have been a greater leaning to steeped pease fried in butter, with pepper and salt. Pancakes so composed passed by the name of *carlings;* and so conspicuous was this article, that from it Carling Sunday became a local name for the day.

> 'Tid, Mid, and Misera,
> *Carling,* Palm, Pase-egg day,'

remains in the north of England as an enumeration of the Sundays of Lent, the first three terms probably taken from words in obsolete services for the respective days, and the fourth being the name of Mid-Lent Sunday from the cakes by which it was distinguished."

Another delicacy much esteemed on "Mothering Sunday" was a simnel cake. Walsh, in *Curiosities of Popular Customs,* says of this dainty: "In Shropshire, Yorkshire and Herefordshire it has long been the custom to make during Lent a cake called a simnel, which is deemed especially appropriate as a 'mothering' present. As far back as Herrick we find

To DIANEME.

A ceremonie in Glocester.
I'll to thee a Sinnell bring,
'Gainst thou go'st a-mothering,
So that when she blesseth thee,
Half that blessing thou'lt give me.

" The inside of a simnel cake was like a rich fruit-cake, but it had an outer crust made of flour and water. Boiled first in water, it was subsequently baked. The crust is colored yellow with saffron and ornamented with more or less art. Professional etymologists refer the word simnel to the Latin *simila,* meaning the finest sort of flour. But folk-etymology declares that the baker-father of Lambert Simnel, pretender to the throne in the reign of Henry VII, was the first to make these cakes, thence called after his own name."

It is a far cry from these quaint English observances of Mid-Lent to our new American festival. We cannot claim for Mothers' Day an unbroken line of descent from the old holiday when English apprentices went " a-mothering." This latest festival of ours is perhaps the most conscious and deliberate effort a nation ever made publicly to honor motherhood and all that it implies.

If the swiftly growing popularity of Mothers' Day shall help to restrain the present tendency towards filial disrespect its emblem, the white carnation, will come to be reverenced as one of the most precious of our national flowers. R. H. S.

NOTE

The Editor, Compiler and Publishers wish to acknowledge their indebtedness to

The Century Company, Clark Austin & Company, T. Y. Crowell & Company, Dodd, Mead & Company, E. P. Dutton & Company, Funk & Wagnalls Company, Houghton Mifflin Company, Harper & Brothers, Little Brown & Company, Jarrold & Sons, The Macmillan Company, A. C. McClurg & Company, Charles Scribner's Sons, World's Best Poetry, and others who have very kindly granted permission to reprint selections from works bearing their copyright.

CONTENTS

CONTENTS

III

CHILD TO MOTHER

CONTENTS

IV

MOTHER TO CHILD

V

MOTHER AND CHILD

CONTENTS

VI

MOTHERS OF THE FAMOUS

CONTENTS

VIII

STORIES

IX

PROGRAMS

CONTENTS

VIII

STORIES

IX

PROGRAMS

I
CELEBRATION

A PROCLAMATION

BY THE PRESIDENT OF THE UNITED STATES OF AMERICA

Whereas, By a Joint Resolution approved May 8, 1914, "designating the second Sunday in May as Mothers' Day, and for other purposes," the President is authorized and requested to issue a proclamation calling upon the government officials to display the United States flag on all government buildings, and the people of the United States to display the flag at their homes or other suitable places on the second Sunday in May as a public expression of our love and reverence for the mothers of our country;

And Whereas, By the said Joint Resolution it is made the duty of the President to request the observance of the second Sunday in May as provided for in the said Joint Resolution:

Now, Therefore, I, Woodrow Wilson, President of the United States of America, by virtue of the authority vested in me by the said Joint Resolution, do hereby direct the government officials to display the United States flag on all government buildings and do invite the people of the United States to display the flag at their homes or other suitable places on the second Sunday in May as a public expression of our love and reverence for the mothers of our country.

In witness whereof I have set my hand and caused the seal of the United States to be hereunto affixed.

Done at the city of Washington this ninth day of May, in the year of our Lord one thousand nine hundred and fourteen, and the Independence of the United States one hundred and thirty-eight.

WOODROW WILSON.

By the President:

WILLIAM JENNINGS BRYAN,
Secretary of State.

(SEAL)

MOTHERS' DAY BILL IN CONGRESS

FROM *Congressional Record,* MAY, 1914

Whereas the service rendered the United States by the American mother is the greatest source of the country's strength and inspiration; and

Whereas we honor ourselves and the mothers of America when we do anything to give emphasis to the home as the fountain head of the State; and

Whereas the American mother is doing so much for the home, for moral uplift, and religion, hence so much for good government and humanity; Therefore be it

Resolved, etc., That the President of the United States is hereby authorized and requested to issue a proclamation calling upon the Government officials to display the United States flag on all Government buildings, and the people of the United States to display the flag at their homes or other suitable places on the second Sunday in May, as a public expression of our love and reverence for the mothers of our country.

Section 2. That the second Sunday in May shall hereafter be designated and known as Mothers' Day, and it shall be the duty of the President to request its observance as provided for in this resolution.

The joint resolution was reported to the Senate as amended and the amendment concurred in.

The amendment was ordered to be engrossed and the joint resolution to be read a third time.

The joint resolution was read a third time and passed.

The preamble was agreed to.

The title was amended to read: " A joint resolution designating the second Sunday in May as Mothers' Day and for other purposes."

A message announced the House agrees with the amendment in joint resolution designating the second Sunday in May as Mothers' Day, and for other purposes.

H. J. Res. 263. Joint resolution designating the second Sunday in May as Mothers' Day, and for other purposes.

Approved and signed by the President. May 8th, 1914.

ORIGIN OF MOTHERS' DAY

By Jane A. Stewart

" I consider the observance of ' Mothers' Day ' one of the most beautiful suggestions I have heard in years. I have adopted it in my own work, and expect after this to have a ' Mothers' Day ' in the campaigns. My own mother has been in heaven for thirty-five years; but her memory is to me most precious, and grows more beautiful with each passing year."

Thus wrote the Reverend Dr. J. Wilbur Chapman, the evangelist, apropos of the annual celebration of the second Sunday of May among churches and Sunday schools as " Mothers' Day " which was started in Philadelphia in 1908.

Many Sunday school associations and young people's societies in all parts of the country have adopted the day, which will be observed by a host of Christian people in 1909. About two hundred thousand, it is estimated, participated in the initial celebration.

The thought of a special " Mothers' Day " in Sunday schools and churches originated with Miss Anna Jarvis, of Philadelphia, to whom the idea came when she was asked by the superintendent of the Sunday-school in the Virginia town in which her deceased mother had long been the moving spirit, to arrange a memorial service.

With the carrying out of this congenial and sacred duty came a realization of the growing lack of tender consideration for absent mothers among worldly-minded, busy, grown-up children; of the thoughtless neglect of home ties and of loving consideration, engendered by the whirl and pressure of modern life; of the lack of respect and deference to parents among children of the present generation; and of the need of a reminder of the loving, unselfish mother, living or dead. And thus the " Mothers' Day " idea came into the churches and Sunday schools, and has been expanded to include an outward demonstration of the latent love and gratitude to mothers, by a gift, words of appreciation, an act of kindness, or a letter, on the part of everybody.

SOME WAYS OF OBSERVING MOTHERS' DAY

By Jane A. Stewart

The services of Mothers' Day as observed in the religious bodies are marked by a deeply religious spirit and earnestness. In the young people's societies and Sunday schools circulars previously distributed are often used to urge every member of the Bible school and church to bring a mother to the special services of the day.

" If your mother be not living, bring some other good mother, one who cannot get to the service without assistance because of infirmity," the invitation reads; and it naturally includes " all mothers, young and old, as guests of honor of the school." Large jars of white carnations ((the floral emblem of mother-love, because of its sweetness, purity and endurance) are set about the platform. These fragrant flowers may be the gift of those who have lost their mothers or of those who wish in this way to show respect and honor to mothers at a distance. And at the close of the exercises one of these white carnations is given to each person present as an appropriate souvenir of Mothers' Day. This distribution of the flowers conducted by the young ushers is an impressive and beautiful feature of the celebration.

The program is naturally varied and impressive. After singing and a prayer, pleading for protection, consideration, and comfort for mothers, a solo is rendered, and some recitations followed by a psalm recited by the school and then a hymn. A brief address by the pastor, perhaps on the text " Honor thy father and thy mother," " The carnation salute," during which the entire audience rises holding aloft bunches of white flowers, followed by the benediction.

An increasing popular plan is to devote the morning service to the Mothers' Day observance, when mother hymns are sung; the pastor preaches a special sermon in recognition of motherhood; and the King's Daughters or similar society, distribute flowers.

The beauty of Christian motherhood is exalted and emphasized by the sweet services of Mothers' Day. The idea of a Mothers' Day has a broad and deep appeal to men as well as women, to rich and poor, to those within and without Christian organizations.

MOTHERS' DAY OBSERVANCE

Mothers' Day was observed in Oklahoma, May 12th, 1912. The proclamation of Gov. Lee Cruce asks that " Each citizen, whether old or young, rich or poor, happy or sorrowful, remember her whose love passeth human understanding, and remembering, manifest to the world your love and gratitude by wearing a carnation in honor of the dearest of all mothers, and, wearing it, think of her and love her."

Olympia, Wash., April 28.—In accordance with a custom that has sprung up all over the United States of setting aside a day for Mothers' Day, Governor M. E. Hay has issued a proclamation naming Sunday, May 8, as Mothers' Day in Washington. He requests that each person wear a white flower on that day and that special religious services be held in all the churches.

The proclamation follows:

> A mother's love — how sweet the name!
>   What is a mother's love?
> A noble, pure and tender flame,
>   Enkindled from above,
> To bless a heart of earthly mold;
>   The warmest love that can grow cold;
> This is a mother's love.

In recent years there has sprung up in many portions of our land a most beautiful custom—that of setting aside one day in the year to be designated as Mothers' Day. Of the many observances we have, there is probably none that appeals more to the average person than this, and as long as this nation shall endure, may this custom never die.

Therefore, in conformance with this usage, I, Marion E. Hay, governor of the State of Washington, do hereby designate and set apart Sunday, May 8, 1910, as Mothers' Day, and do recommend and request that it be observed as such throughout this commonwealth. I urge that, on that day, all persons wear a white flower in acknowledgment and honor of the one who went down into the valley of the shadow of death for us. No more fitting place can be found for holding special services of this character than in our churches, and I request that all religious organizations throughout our State prepare a special program for this day, and I urge all good citizens to attend these services.

MOTHERS' DAY OBSERVANCE IN SEATTLE, 1910

From a Seattle Newspaper

Within the past two years America has imported an established English custom, that of setting aside the second Sunday in May as " Mothers' Day " and this year the churches, without regard to denomination, will use for their dominant sentiment the glory of motherhood and will exert every effort to make the day a time of tender remembrance.

The observance was first advocated in this country last year by the Presbyterian assembly. This year other denominations have taken the matter up, and through their assemblies and local church circles it is expected that more than fifty Seattle pastors will give the subject prominence in the services to-morrow.

The call to observe the day is directed by the Presbyterian committee to the men particularly. Each man is asked to write a letter to his mother, if absent, tell her in person he loves her if she is living, and if she is dead, to wear a white carnation as a token of remembrance. The ladies are requested to bring bouquets of flowers as the outward expression of a similar sentiment.

Following last year's precedent, the First Presbyterian Church in Seattle will make the floral offerings the subject of a special ceremony at the services at 11 A. M. to-morrow. At a given signal from Rev. M. A. Matthews, the pastor, all the women are to hold their bouquets aloft while the pastor pronounces a blessing, and at the close of the services the flowers will be gathered and placed on the graves of mothers whose relatives are not in the city to perform the duty.

II

MOTHERHOOD

AN ENGLISH MOTHER

By ROBERT UNDERWOOD JOHNSON *

Every week of every season out of English ports go
    forth,
White of sail or white of trail, East, or West, or
    South, or North,
Scattering like a flight of pigeons, half a hundred
    home-sick ships,
Bearing half a hundred striplings — each with kisses
    on his lips
Of some silent mother, fearful lest she shows herself
    too fond,
Giving him to bush or desert as one pays a sacred
    bond,
— Tell us, you who hide your heartbreak, which is
    sadder, when all's done,
To repine an English mother, or to roam, an English
    son?

You who shared your babe's first sorrow when his
    cheek no longer pressed
On the perfect, snow-and-roseleaf beauty of your
    mother-breast,
In the rigor of his nurture was your woman's mercy
    mute,
Knowing he was doomed to exile with the savage and
    the brute?

Did you school yourself to absence all his adolescent
  years,
That, though you be torn with parting, he should never
  see the tears?
Now his ship has left the offing for the many-mouthèd
  sea,
This your guerdon, empty heart, by empty bed to bend
  the knee!

And if he be but the latest thus to leave your dwin-
  dling board,
Is a sorrow less for being added to a sorrow's hoard?
Is the mother-pain the duller that to-day his brothers
  stand,
Facing ambuscades of Congo, or alarms from Zulu-
  land?
Toil, where blizzards drift the snow like smoke across
  the plains of death?
Faint, where tropic fens at morning steam with fever-
  laden breath?
Die, that in some distant river's veins the English
  blood may run —
Mississippi, Yangtze, Ganges, Nile, Mackenzie, Ama-
  zon?

Ah! you still must wait and suffer in a solitude un-
  told
While your sisters of the nations call you passive, call
  you cold —
Still must scan the news of sailings, breathless search
  the slow gazette,

Find the dreadful name . . . and, later, get his blithe
    farewell! And yet —
Shall the lonely hearthstone shame the legions who
    have died
Grudging not the price their country pays for progress
    and for pride?
— Nay; but, England, do not ask us thus to emulate
    your scars
Until women's tears are reckoned in the budgets of
    your wars.

*From the fourth edition of the author's "Collected Poems, Saint-Gaudens; an Ode, and Other Poems." Copyright 1913 by Robert Underwood Johnson. New York and Indianapolis: The Bobbs-Merrill Co.

QUOTATIONS

Then spake the woman whose the living child was
unto the king, for her bowels yearned upon her son,
and she said, O my lord, give her the living child, and
in no wise slay it. But the other said, Let it be neither
mine nor thine, but divide it.

Then the king answered and said, Give her the living child, and in no wise slay it: she is the mother
thereof.

I KINGS, iii, 26, 27.

When Jesus therefore saw his mother, and the
disciple standing by, whom he loved, he said unto his
mother, Woman, behold thy son!

Then saith he to the disciple, Behold thy mother!
and from that hour that disciple took her unto his own
home.

ST. JOHN, xix, 26, 27.

And it came to pass the day after, that he went into a city called Nain: and many of his disciples went with him, and much people.

Now when he came nigh to the gate of the city, behold, there was a dead man carried out, the only son of his mother, and she was a widow: and much people of the city was with her.

And when the Lord saw her, he had compassion on her, and said unto her, Weep not.

And he came and touched the bier: and they that bare him stood still. And he said, Young man, I say unto thee, Arise.

And he that was dead sat up, and began to speak: and he delivered him to his mother.

And there came a fear on all: and they glorified God.

St. LUKE, vii, 11, 12, 13, 14, 15.

And when she could not longer hide him, she took for him an ark of bulrushes, and daubed it with slime and with pitch, and put the child therein; and she laid it in the flags by the river's brink.

EXODUS, ii, 3.

Many make the household but only one the home.

JAMES RUSSELL LOWELL.

Youth fades, love droops, the leaves of friendship fall;
A mother's secret hope outlives them all.

N. P. WILLIS.

They say that man is mighty,
  He govern' land and sea,
He wields a mighty scepter
  O'er lesser powers than he;

But mightier power and stronger
  Man from his throne has hurled,
For the hand that rocks the cradle
  Is the hand that rules the world.

W. R. WALLACE.

AS AT THY PORTALS ALSO DEATH

BY WALT WHITMAN *

As at thy portals also death,
Entering thy sovereign, dim, illimitable grounds,
To memories of my mother, to the divine blending,
    maternity,
To her buried and gone, yet buried not, gone not from
    me,
(I see again the calm benignant face fresh and beau-
    tiful still,
I sit by the form in the coffin,
I kiss and kiss convulsively again the sweet old lips,
    the cheeks, the closed eyes in the coffin;)
To her, the ideal woman, practical, spiritual, of all of
    earth, life, love, to me the best,
I grave a monumental line, before I go, amid these
    songs,
And set a tombstone here.

By courtesy of the Walter Scott Company, Limited.

OLD MOTHERS

BY CHARLES S. ROSS

I love old mothers — mothers with white hair,
And kindly eyes, and lips grown softly sweet,

With murmured blessings over sleeping babes.
There is a something in their quiet grace
That speaks the calm of Sabbath afternoons;
A knowledge in their deep, unfaltering eyes,
That far outreaches all philosophy.

Time with caressing touch, about them weaves
The silver-threaded fairy-shawl of age,
While all the echoes of forgotten songs
Seemed joined to lend a sweetness to their speech.

Old mothers! — as they pass with slow-timed step,
Their trembling hands cling gently to youth's strength.
Sweet mothers! as they pass, one sees again,
Old garden walks, old roses, and old loves.

MOTHERS AND MOTHERHOOD

FROM *Best Thoughts of Best Thinkers*

There is a Jewish saying that " God could not be everywhere and therefore he made mothers."

While this saying may conflict with our ideas concerning omnipresence as a necessary attribute of Deity, it nevertheless voices an essential truth, that mothers, as the representatives of the fecundity of nature, sustain the closest relation to God as his chosen channel through which to manifest the highest forms of creative power. " The fatherhood of God, the motherhood of nature and the consequent brotherhood of man," is an expression giving motherhood almost coördinate rank with God, and harmonizes perfectly with Bulwer Lytton's well known expression, " Nature's loving proxy, the watchful mother." The " proxy " idea grows out of the fact that the mother's instincts, acting as they do independently of and prior to reason, and being superior to and disconnected from the understanding, are in close and vital touch with the infinite source of all wisdom, and hence a substitute for God within the limitations of their function.

While it is true that highly educated mothers have written most feelingly of motherhood it is also true that the best thinkers among men in all ages have acknowledged the supremacy of the maternal tie, often ascribing divine attributes to her surpassing tenderness. Michelet says, " It is the general rule, that all superior men inherit the elements of their superiority from their mothers." To this add the words of the immortal Lincoln, " All that I am, or hope to be, I owe to my angel mother"; and the tribute of John Quincy Adams, " All that I am my mother made me." Such acknowledgments can be duplicated over and over again from the literature of all countries and all times. Thus Napoleon, " The future of the child is always the work of the mother"; and again, Napoleon, " Let France have good mothers and she will have good sons."

Longfellow drawing his inspiration from the contemplation of motherhood says, ".Even He that died for us upon the cross, in the last hour, in the unutterable agony of death, was mindful of His mother, as if to teach us that this holy love should be our last worldly thought, the last point of earth from which the soul should take its flight for heaven."

MY MOTHER

By William Bell Scott *

There was a gather'd stillness in the room:
Only the breathing of the great sea rose
From far off, aiding that profound repose,
With regular pulse and pause within the gloom
Of twilight, as if some impending doom
Was now approaching; — I sat moveless there,
Watching with tears and thoughts that were like
　　prayer,
Till the hour struck,— the thread dropp'd from the
　　loom;
And the Bark pass'd in which freed souls are borne.
The dear still'd face lay there; that sound forlorn
Continued; I rose not, but long sat by:
And now my heart oft hears that sad sea-shore,
When she is in the far-off land, and I
Wait the dark sail returning yet once more.

　* From " The Victorian Anthology." Houghton Mifflin Company.

MOTHER AND CHILD

By William Gilmore Simms

The wind blew wide the casement, and within —
It was the loveliest picture! — a sweet child
Lay in its mother's arms, and drew its life,

In pauses, from the fountain,— the white round
Part shaded by loose tresses, soft and dark,
Concealing, but still showing, the fair realm
Of so much rapture, as green shadowing trees
With beauty shroud the brooklet. The red lips
Were parted, and the cheek upon the breast
Lay close, and, like the young leaf of the flower,
Wore the same color, rich and warm and fresh: —
And such alone are beautiful. Its eye,
A full blue gem, most exquisitely set,
Looked archly on its world,— the little imp,
As if it knew even then that such a wreath
Were not for all; and with its playful hands
It drew aside the robe that hid its realm,
And peeped and laughed aloud, and so it laid
Its head upon the shrine of such pure joys,
And, laughing, slept. And while it slept, the tears
Of the sweet mother fell upon its cheek,—
Tears such as fall from April skies, and bring
The sunlight after. They were tears of joy;
And the true heart of that young mother then
Grew lighter, and she sang unconsciously
The silliest ballad-song that ever yet
Subdued the nursery's voices, and brought sleep
To fold her sabbath wings above its couch.

PENSIONING MOTHERS

From *The Literary Digest*

In spite of a good deal of sincere opposition from
charity workers and philanthropic organizations, the

socialistic device of State " pensions " for indigent mothers is making remarkable headway in the legislatures and is being received with very general favor by the press.

The Illinois " Mothers' Compensation law " was enacted in 1911. In November, 1912, a writer in *The World's Work* reported the following facts concerning its operation:

" The Cook County Juvenile Court, in the city of Chicago last summer, had some 327 mothers, with an aggregate of 1,200 children, cared for on this plan. (Funds for Parents or Mother's Pension Act.) It is costing the community an average of $5.75 per month per child, as against $10 per month per child under the old institutional plan.

It will cost the State of Illinois this year about $100,000. Eventually when enough mothers have learned about it, that figure, it is expected, will rise to $200,000. The State authorities have said that they do not care if it goes to $500,000. The contract with the mothers will be cheap at that. For it is counted on to diminish the bill for crime that is now costing Cook County alone $6,000,000 a year."

The same writer added:

" Working mothers and the consequent lack of care are what has sent many of the city children on the way toward failure in life. The child that does not have enough of his mother is likely to get that way. The institutional child, separated entirely from her, is more than likely to. Statistics from the Elmira

Reformatory in New York State show that 60 per cent. of the inmates were brought up in institutions. Of four young men hanged in Cook County, Illinois, early in 1912, all had been raised in charitable or reformatory institutions. The motherhood pension way is to form children by home raising so that they will not have to be reformed."

Colorado's Mothers' Compensation Law, which was put on the statute book at the recent election by a referendum vote of the people, does not differ materially from the Illinois law. It provides, writes George Creel in the Denver *Rocky Mountain News,* that " the State may award money to widowed and indigent mothers for the support of children in the home." Mr. Creel, who, with Judge Ben B. Lindsey, was one of the chief sponsors of the bill, points out that " it is not only good Christianity, but good business." He says :

" For one-third of the money that it takes to keep a child in an institution, that child can be kept at home. And who will say that a ' home ' child is not better off than an ' institution ' child ? "

The last clause of the Colorado law provides that it " shall be liberally construed for the protection of the child, the home, and the State, and the interests of public morals, and for the prevention of poverty and crime."

The Newark *Monitor* is inclined to think that the idea of State pensions for mothers " rests on sound social and business principles." A measure sanctioned by both sentiment and economy, it says, is at least worthy of careful study. The movement, remarks the Spokane *Spokesman Review,* is "an expression of the new social consciousness," and "has taken firm hold on popular sympathy." Under the present system in Ohio, remarks the Columbus *Citizen,* the indigent mother whose husband has died or deserted her has choice of three things —

"1. She may give her children up, place them in an orphan's home, and go in the bleak desolation of bereaved motherhood about her dreary task of keeping body and soul together.

"2. She may strive to keep the children at home, and leave their lives to chance while she labors, away from them, 10, 12, 14 hours a day, returning only in time to place them in their beds.

"3. She may STAY AT HOME WITH THEM AND STARVE."

"We have waited long enough," exclaims the *Citizen,* "for legislation to remedy these conditions."

The Ohio law, we are informed by the press, provides for pensions of $15 a month to dependent widows with one child under fourteen, and to mothers with one child under fourteen whose husbands are helpless or in prison, or who have abandoned their families. There is an extra pension of $7 a month for each additional child under fourteen years. The court, we read further, "must satisfy itself that the child is living with its mother, that without the pension the home would be broken up, that it is beneficial to the child to stay with its mother and, after investigation, that the home is a proper one." This mothers' aid measure, the Cincinnati *Enquirer* notes, "is really an extensive codification of the juvenile delinquency laws and a revision of acts relating to children's homes, occupations of youths, and the management and direction of private and public orphan asylums and refuges. Its ramifications are extensive and will affect many industries employing females under twenty-one years of age and males under eighteen."

Such aid to mothers, explains the New York *World* in its news columns, "is a tax payers' money saver, while increasing the self-respect of both mothers and children." The expensive supervision in State institutions is replaced by the home supervision of the mothers.

Yet the New York *Times* points to the allegations of weaknesses in the workings of the motherhood pension law in Illinois, the pioneer State in this movement. And the Brooklyn *Eagle,* discussing the proposals for similar legislation in New York, believes that though "the pension system, according to the theorists, is better than any other plan of relief," it probably "never could be carefully administered and the opportunity for extravagance developed from sentimentalism is gravely apparent." Objection to the description of this reform as "mothers' or widows' pensions" is made by the New York *Evening Post.*

"Motherhood has not been endowed," it carefully explains: "The State is merely giving assistance to needy children and older persons while allowing them to remain at home, instead of following the more usual procedure of putting them into an institution. The 'pensions' are not to be spent at the free will of those who receive them, as an old soldier may spend his, but under strict regulation by the courts. They are payments for certain purposes rather than pensions. For such an arrangement there is much to be said. Where a mother has the strength and the capacity to take care of her children, but cannot do so if she must employ her time away from home in earning their bread, it is surely wiser to give her the money that will enable her to make useful citizens out of her children, than to turn them over to professional caretakers, however worthy the latter may be. Nor will there be any objection to such payments to indigent widows without children as will keep soul and body together, if the whole matter is carefully supervised. Preservation of the home is worth all it may cost in this way. But let us not carelessly talk as if a new and large section of society were about to be pensioned for life."

The following States have adopted the pensioning of mothers, 1915:

Arizona	Missouri	Oregon
California	Nebraska	Pennsylvania
Idaho	Nevada	South Dakota
Iowa	New Hampshire	Utah
Illinois	New Jersey	Washington
Massachusetts	New York	Wisconsin
Michigan	Ohio	
Minnesota	Oklahoma	

SEVEN TIMES SIX. GIVING IN MARRIAGE

By Jean Ingelow

To bear, to nurse, to rear,
　To watch, and then to lose:
To see my bright ones disappear,
　Drawn up like morning dews,—
To bear, to nurse, to rear,
　To watch and then to lose:
This have I done when God drew near
　Among his own to choose.

To hear, to heed, to wed,
　And with thy lord depart
In tears that he, as soon as shed,
　Will let no longer smart,—
To hear to heed, to wed,
　This while thou didst I smiled,
For now it was not God who said,
　" Mother, give me thy child."

O fond, O fool, and blind,
　To God I gave with tears,
But when a man like grace would find,
　My soul put by her fears,—
O, fond, O fool, and blind,
　God guards in happier spheres;
That man will guard where he did bind
　Is hope for unknown years.

To hear, to heed, to wed,
  Fair lot that maidens choose,
Thy mother's tenderest words are said,
  Thy face no more she views;
Thy mother's lot, my dear,
  She doth in nought accuse;
Her lot to bear, to nurse, to rear,
  To love,— and then to lose.

LITTLE MOTHERS

By S. T. R.

To-day everything is being done for the child.   The child is the hope of the race — the father and mother of the next generation.

The children of the poor though were long left, in the great cities, to grow up as best they could, but now that modern living with its improved conditions of work has given woman a chance to reach out and make the world her household, the little people are claiming the attention of the Mother Spirit that is abroad.   Now it is realized how important is the child of the poor and how that life can be nourished and inspired and some joy and childhood given it.

Children love their dolls.   The mother instinct is early shown both in girls and boys.   The boy is quickly laughed out of it but often a teddy-bear is still allowed him and is as consoling for all hours of the day and night as the doll is to the girl.   Alas, if people were wiser, and let this gentleness and love have full play, there might be reared men who would have a deeper love and responsibility for their children. The father instinct is so often crushed.

Among the poor, dolls and the time to play with dolls, are not to be had. But there is sure to be a baby in the family on whom the devotion that is lavished, by a sister, only a little older, has given these caretaking children the name of " Little Mothers."

One day Mrs. Alma Calder Johnston looking from her window in Stuyvesant Square, saw little girls carrying babies in their arms, all too heavy for such children. She found these little girls were taking care of their baby brothers and sisters while their mothers were away all day earning a living for the family. Here they were, losing all mothering themselves — what could be done to restore to them their childhood?

Mrs. Johnston began by taking small parties of these children, for days' outings, to the country.

So the " Little Mothers' " Aid began in 1899 until to-day we find the Association with four houses, with day nurseries. Classes in cooking, sewing, laundry, hygiene, and dress-making are taught every day to these children cut off from ordinary schools by their home cares.

And not only this, but the workers from the Aid go out into the homes and while the big mothers are gone to work, make the tenement clean and liveable so that the family can be kept together.

In some of these homes are crippled children. Busy doctors give hours every week to relieving their suffering.

Do not the names of these four houses for little girls and babies, suggest the joy that has come into the little mothers' lives? "Happy Day House," "Pleasant Place," "Loving Arms," "Sunny Side."

And for summer where thousands go in relays from week to week "Holiday House."

To these houses kind friends send money, clothing, books, and toys, for all are supported by contributions. Other kind friends serve as officers, teachers, and nurses. And children of all nationalities and all faiths spend hours, of work and play, together under this beautiful charity to "the least of these."

"SHE MADE HOME HAPPY"

BY HENRY COYLE

"She made home happy!" these few words I read
 Within a churchyard, written on a stone;
 No name, no date, the simple words alone,
Told me the story of the unknown dead.
A marble column lifted high its head
 Close by, inscribed to one the world has known;
 But ah! that lonely grave with moss o'ergrown
Thrilled me far more than his who armies led.

"She made home happy!" through the long sad years,
 The mother toiled and never stopped to rest,
 Until they crossed her hands upon her breast,
And closed her eyes, no longer dim with tears.
The simple record that she left behind
 Was grander than the soldier's to my mind.

LITTLE MOTHERS

By Emma S. Nesfield *

Sometimes in this queer old world, blessings are thrust upon us, and we simply take them for granted — accept them as our right — and think no more about them. One of the most common of these are the Little Mothers. Nearly every large-sized or even moderately large-sized family, and oftentimes just ordinary little families have one. Sometimes they don't even know they have them, because these precious blessings are born, like every other baby, and by the time they have seriously taken up their life-work, why, they are just one of the family.

Once there was a really large, old-fashioned family of five boys and four girls, and the second girl, who happened to be the third baby, was one of those things I've been telling you about. She wasn't particularly strong in body — very often they are not — but she made up for it in mind, in love, in sympathy, in all the golden abstractions of true womanhood.

In the beginning of the story, the family was very prosperous but like many large, old-fashioned, high-principled families, each year saw prosperity fading away into the dim and distant " used to be's." So, by the time this Little Mother was well on in her work, the world at large seemed to be one big, strug-gling, strangling problem.

When the last baby came, the Real Mother of the family somehow did not have the strength to go on struggling, and though life meant very much to her, though her work was waiting for her, giving the little new baby to her oldest girl, she stopped living.

This oldest girl, like many another girl, scarce grown, stepped into her mother's place. She washed and combed, dressed and prayed over the little ones. She managed on narrow margin to keep the large family together, with a fair amount of the happiness and good times that always come to large families, even under the most distressing pressures. And when her little charges were well on their way: when the older ones were prepared to begin life's work — to swell the little margin to comfortable appearances — a big, lonely, homeless man came and begged her to help him gather Household Gods.

Then the Little Mother took the helm. Somehow, it seemed natural. For ever so long, " the boys," now big brothers, had been coming to her for sympathy — for advice, which was mostly so good that it was seldom acted on — for comfort, when misfortune followed failure, to be advised. And they never found her wanting; because being what she was, she could not help herself. She often scolded them with righteous indignation, and then relented of her cruelty in tears. How those brothers loved her of all the sisters; how they pained her most, is only a repetition of what always happens to her kind.

One by one the brothers and sisters married, started new circles, named new babies for this well-beloved sister, and had her godmother the new-comers. While she just struggled on trying to make ends meet as a reduced gentlelady only can, by teaching petted darlings of the moneyed people in the world; and by giving readings and lectures to small seekers after culture.

At last one day a cold gripped her with a merciless hold, and she, having nothing left to struggle for — no more mothering to do — had not the strength to fight it off. When they had buried her by her father and mother, and left her forever, to go back to their world of husbands and wives and babies, then this family realized, for the first time, that God had sent them a " Little Mother " and they had not known it; had taken her for granted until she was gone — and her life had been only half lived.

But that is the way with " Little Mothers." You will find them the world over, in the tenements and the alleys, in the palaces and mansions. They give all they have. They worry and they grieve, comfort and scold, shield and protect, and when they have nothing left to mother, they mostly die. For, after all, they are blessings thrust upon us, and we simply take them for granted — accept them as our right — and think no more about them, giving them belated appreciation when they are gone.

By courtesy of the Overland Monthly.

MATRES DOLOROSAE

By Robert Bridges *

Ye Spartan mothers, gentle ones,
Of lion-hearted, loving sons,

Fal'n, the flower of English youth,
To a barbarous foe in a land uncouth: —

O what a delicate sacrifice!
Unequal the stake and costly the price
As when the queen of Love deplor'd
Her darling by the wild-beast gor'd.

They rode to war as if to the hunt,
But ye at home, ye bore the brunt,
Bore the siege of torturing fears,
Fed your hope on the bread of tears.

Proud and spotless warriors they
With love or sword to lead the way;
For ye had cradled heart and hand,
The commander harken'd to your command.

Ah, weeping mothers, now all is o'er,
Ye know your honor and mourn no more:
Nor ask ye a name in England's story,
Who gave your dearest for her glory.

May 20, 1902.

* From the one volume edition of the Works of Robert Bridges. Oxford University Press, by permission of the author.

MATERNITY

By Anne P. L. Field

Within the crib that stands beside my bed
    A little form in sweet abandon lies
    And as I bend above with misty eyes
I know how Mary's heart was comforted.

O world of Mothers! blest are we who know
   The ecstasy — the deep God-given thrill
   That Mary felt when all the earth was still
In the Judean starlight long ago!

" MOTHER "

A Review by George Middleton

Occasionally there comes along a book which for
sheer beauty demands merely a record of its recogni-
tion rather than an extended review that might con-
tain presumptive criticism. Mrs. Norris in *Mother*
has produced just such a little story: its charm of
treatment dignifying the old theme about which it is
written. It seems only a frail story in outline yet it
reflects so much observation of the tiny facets of hu-
man nature that it will, no doubt, float happily by a
long stream of readers. Boss Tweed said he did not
care what was written about him only he could not
stand the cartoons. *Mother* suggests, in its picture
of what is thought to be old-fashioned motherhood,
more by the persuasion of its own beauty, the neces-
sity of such an ideal, than all the theoretical discus-
sions of motherhood from the statistical and socio-
logical standpoint. And yet, granting this, we can-
not help feeling while it moves us to tears and so
serves its purpose of spiritualizing our innate love of all
mothers, that it remains only a picture — something
we would wish to hang in the gallery of our dearest
wishes, possible to realize only in certain tempera-

ments, not a conclusion or final statement of what should be or can be brought about in our economic scheme. Mothers *are* and are not made: motherhood is so often functional, accidental, and not a profession, as Mrs. Paget makes it. The restlessness of so many women, under modern conditions, cannot find its expression in family life, like the Pagets, and we are not sure the forceful utterances of men against "race suicide" and unbearing wives, or the more subtle delicate protests of such writers as Mrs. Norris, are not a bit unjust and uncomprehending. The boy of this large family is due to an idealized mother, but, unfortunately, successful motherhood, like wifehood from which it so often differs, is a distinct vocation, and if this story be the protest it seems at our own apparent lack of such mothers and families, the answer lies in the region of each feminine temperament backed and altered as it has had to be by our varying environments.

But certainly *Mother* does reveal the deep chasm which exists between the real homespun mother, like Mrs. Paget with her seven children, and the satin-lined mothers who waddle talkatively amid trained nurses, bridge-tables, and a stray Fauntleroyed boy. Margaret, Mrs. Paget's daughter, whose experiences form the thin line of the story, discovers there is a lot of social inconvenience in bringing children into the world, and we are glad such mothers as Mrs. Carr-Boldt limit the supply; only when she returns to her own mother, with a man's love awakening her own instinctive reach for children, does she get her true values and sees it is externals which have been most at fault in the other world. It is a delicate passage, indeed, where she sheds all the verbal fungus about love, marriage and children she has acquired as a rich woman's secretary, and stands naked before her own need. Here Mrs. Norris has touched highwater mark with an intimate understanding of all that is elusive and all that is bold when love speaks. Then Margaret reads a rhythm into what seemed commonplaceness, the sordidness and care of her mother's life, which has been so repellent to her, and she finds, too, how the joy of motherhood for its own sake is its own compensation, giving a selfish satisfaction to what many would call sacrifice.

And Margaret had sometimes wished, or half formed the wish, that she and Bruce had been the only ones — Good God! that was what women did, then, when they denied the right of life to the distant, unwanted, possible little person! Calmly, constantly, in all placid philosophy and self-justification, they kept from the world — not only the troublesome new baby, with his tears and illness, his merciless exactions, his endless claim on mind and body and spirit — but perhaps the glowing beauty of a Rebecca, the buoyant, indomitable spirit of a Leo, the sturdy charm of a small Robert, whose grip on life, whose energy and ambition were as strong as Margaret's own! Margaret stirred uneasily, frowned in the dark. It seemed perfectly incredible, it seemed perfectly *impossible* that if Mother had had only two — and how many thousands of women didn't have that! — she, Margaret, a pronounced and separate entity, traveled, ambitious, and to be the wife of one of the world's great men, might not have been lying here in the summer night, rich in love and youth and beauty and her dreams!

THE BABY

By Jane Taylor

Safe sleeping on its mother's breast
　The smiling babe appears,
Now sweetly sinking into rest;
　Now washed in sudden tears:
Hush, hush, my little baby dear,
There's nobody to hurt you here.

Without a mother's tender care,
　The little thing must die,
Its chubby hands too feeble are
　One service to supply;
And not a tittle does it know
What kind of world 't is come into.

The lambs sport gaily on the grass
　When scarcely born a day;
The foal, beside its mother ass,
　Trots frolicksome away,
No other creature, tame or wild,
Is half so helpless as a child.

To nurse the Dolly, gaily drest,
　And stroke its flaxen hair,

Or ring the coral at its waist,
  With silver bells so fair,
Is all the little creature can,
That is so soon to be a man.

Full many a summer's sun must glow
  And lighten up the skies,
Before its tender limbs can grow
  To anything of size;
And all the while the mother's eye
Must every little want supply.

Then surely, when each little limb
  Shall grow to healthy size,
And youth and manhood strengthen him
  For toil and enterprise,
His mother's kindness is a debt,
He never, never will forget.

THE MOTHER IN DRAMA

By Henry Barrett Hinckley

In no period of the drama in Europe does motherhood seem frequently to have been an important theme. Numerous dramatic situations where motherhood is an essential motive might have been devised. And indeed the frequency with which the slaying of Clytemnestra by her children has been made the subject of a play,— there are not less than nine *Electras* in Greek, Latin and French alone — shows that the theme has certainly its appeal. Yet for some reason situations and plots involving motherhood are rather rare in the literature of the stage. And no satisfactory explanation of the fact has occurred to me.

Homer has left us two striking pictures of motherhood, one where Hecuba on the wall implores her son Hector to come inside the city and avoid the onset of Achilles, the other where Andromache and her little son Astyanax take leave of Hector ere he goes to battle. This latter has ever been justly conceded to be one of the truest and most beautiful of all pictures of domestic affection and it might seem as if the Attic dramatists would often have vied with it. But the position of woman in the great days of Athens was lower than in the Homeric age, and tender motherhood is by no means a conspicuous theme of the tragedians even in Euripides. In the Agamemnon of Aeschylus, Clytemnestra, with majestic insolence and withering scorn, refers to the daughter whom her husband sacrificed at Aulis, and whose shade will meet him and kiss him in the world below. Among the titles of lost dramas none is more tantalizing than the *Niobe,* found among the fragments both of Aeschylus and of Sophocles, but it is impossible from the few extant lines to form any idea how either dramatist developed the character of the mother whose pride drew the vengeance of the gods. Clytemnestra and Medea are both vengeful murderesses, though the art of the dramatist keeps them human. But Euripides, in his *Women of Troy,* harking back to Homer, has given us far and away the most affecting picture of mother-

hood ever presented on the stage of antiquity. Here
are Andromache and Astyanax essentially as in Ho-
mer, but now the evil day of slavery has befallen them.
The play lacks unity. But it contains some of Euri-
pides' thoroughly representative work, expressing
with tender beauty his characteristic sympathy for the
weak, the helpless, the disregarded. Even here,
though Hector is dead, Andromache is pictured largely
as the faithful and devoted wife, observant of every
least propriety toward her husband. But the climax
expresses her feelings when she takes leave of her
child, whom the Greeks have decided to slay, lest he
should become a second Hector. Talthybius, who in-
forms her of the decision of the Greeks, does his cruel
errand as humanely as the terrible circumstances will
allow, especially cautioning Andromache not to re-
sist, nor to utter any execrations lest the Greeks after
slaying the child should leave its corpse unburied —
a horrible thing according to Greek ideas. The situa-
tion will remind every reader of Chaucer's Griselda
being deprived of her babes. Andromache's farewell
begins with splendid dignity and self-command. To-
ward the end she does give way to some ejacula-
tions which apparently Talthybius is considerate
enough not to repeat to the Greeks; for the little body
is returned for burial. The play was written in 415
B. C., in the midst of the great Peloponnesian War, and
it is hard not to believe that Euripides desired princi-
pally to give a picture of the sufferings that war brings
upon women, and especially upon mothers. It is one
of those extraordinary works in which Euripides ex-

presses the living sentiments of our own day. And he brings to the treatment of his theme a daring intelligence no less than his extraordinary power of expressing the tender and the pathetic. He boldly fastens the responsibility for the terrible Trojan war on Helen, denying that the gods had anything to do with it.

Euripides had advanced ideas on the responsibilities of parents, but their most striking expression is found in connection with fatherhood. In the *Ion* there is a noble and elevated discourse on paternity, arraigning Apollo for deserting his child by a mortal mother. Of course conservative Athenians thought this accusation of a god to be a terrible impiety. But Euripides is everywhere possessed by an exalted sense of social justice, penetrating the cruel conventions of his age; an ethical insight which was long unequaled in literature. He thought earnestly as well as felt. Of all men of the ancient world he was the most modern in his moral ideals. Beside the Andromache, already described, he has left us a noble picture of motherhood in Alcestis who voluntarily surrendered herself to the grim specter Death in order that her husband Admetus might live. It is difficult for the modern reader to value Admetus, who too complacently accepts her sacrifice, except as a foil to his brave and generous wife. But the play was intended to celebrate the hospitality of Admetus who by receiving, even in this hour of bereavement, the hero Hercules as a guest receives as a reward Alcestis back from the grave, Hercules having wrestled with Death himself for her deliverance. But it is Alcestis who gives to the play its undying glory, and nowhere is she more glorious than in commending her children to her husband just before she dies.

The Romans, in their better days, had a higher respect for women than had the Athenians, but the drama of Rome is too unoriginal in character to detain us. Shakespeare has left us a number of pictures of mothers. Lady Capulet is but slightly sketched, and in a comic spirit. There are several mothers in the ranting chronicle plays of *Henry VI,* such as Elizabeth of York and Margaret of Anjou. Of later date, yet not free from the blustering manner of these earlier plays, is the Constance in the play of *King John,* the mother of John's nephew and rival, Prince Arthur, a gentle and affectionate lad, destitute of the powerful energy and ambition which alone could have won him the crown of England and thereby saved his life from his wicked uncle. The task of upholding his cause devolves upon his mother, who pleads his cause before the King of France, and the archduke of Austria with courage, with pride, and alas with bitterness. Majestic and pathetic as she is, she has no arts of diplomacy or persuasion. With an irrepressible pride that cannot recognize defeat, she asserts her son's dignity, with stormy eloquence, but without useful result. The scenes in which she and Eleanor, the mother and champion of King John, scold each other are in the ranting vein of Marlowe. Shakespeare may not have written all of the play as it has reached us, or if he did, his genius had by no means ripened.

It is interesting to find that the most delicately beautiful lines in the play, the dialogue between Arthur and Hubert, and the elegant compliment beginning

To gild refinèd gold, to paint the lily,

are spoken by men and not by women. Shakespeare had hardly yet associated with high-bred women. He was more impressed with the dramatic possibilities of the village goodies who sat in the dust and scolded each other with all possible intemperance.

Gertrude, the mother of Hamlet, on the other hand, is a finished and masterly portrait. She has been unfaithful to her husband during his life, though not an accessory before the fact of his murder. Her easy self-indulgent nature readily persuades her that now she has married her paramour, Hamlet's uncle, the past is of little import. But though destitute of moral ideals, she is by no means destitute of attractive sentiment. Her fidelity to her son is a main embarrassment to her husband. Her affection for Ophelia is wholly sweet and pleasing. Her insensibility to the merits of her first husband, the father whose memory Hamlet so passionately revered and loved, is the source of the heavy cloud that rests upon the soul of the Prince of Denmark, inhibiting his will, and deranging his intellect. For modern literature contains no more beautiful picture of moral sensibility than Hamlet. But when at last he succeeds in rousing the slumbering conscience of his mother, she unhesitatingly espouses his cause, keeps his confidence, and perishes with his name upon her lips.

Volumnia, the mother of Coriolanus, is the most motherly, in her stern, antique Roman way, of all Shakespeare's portraits of motherhood. Hardly less intense than the Constance already mentioned, Volumnia is vastly more real; for she is no merely animated form of a single passion, but a human being moved by patrician pride, and by steadfast patriotism as well as by maternal ambition. Occasionally, too, she shows a flash of penetrating intelligence, particularly when she directs her son how to assume the appearance of humility in the presence of the plebeians whom both mother and son really despise:

> Thy knee bussing the stones — for in such business
> Action is eloquence, and the eyes of the ignorant
> More learned than their ears —

The haughty patrician cannot understand kindness to a lower caste. But she knows their weakness, and knows, too, how to make her exhortations all but persuasive to her incorrigible son. The character of Volumnia is a truly admirable example of Shakespeare's historic sense, showing how genius, aided by small Latin and less Greek — for he never went beyond North's translation of Plutarch for his story — can catch the spirit of one who lived in a distant age.

The age of Coriolanus and Volumnia was one of very simple militarism. Volumnia's every boast is of her son's physical courage and strength. Living in our own age of feminism she would have been the first to proclaim that great men have great mothers.

" Thy valiantness was mine, thou suck'dst it from

me," she says.   She glories even in her son's wounds,
being intellectual enough to regard them as mere evi-
dence of his greatness: " O he is wounded; I thank
the gods for it," she cries, for " On's brows he comes
the third time home with the oaken garland."   She
also boasts of her grandson: " He had rather see the
swords and hear a drum beat than look upon his school-
master."   But underneath the haughty spirit that ever
values her son's glory more than his safety there is ever
the insistent fondness of a mother.   This is expressed
to the life when kneeling before him " with no softer
cushion than the flint " she implores him to spare his
native city, now at his mercy:

> Thou hast never in thy life
> Show'd thy dear mother any courtesy,
> When she, poor hen, fond of no second brood,
> Has cluck'd thee to the wars and safely home,
> Loaden with honor.

An interesting picture of a woman who has spoiled her
son not by cosseting or softening him, but by inflam-
ing his pride and his courage.

In recent drama, the German, Gerhart Hauptmann,
has given us a powerful play in *The Rats*.   There is a
double plot of which only one part, the tragedy of
Mrs. John, the mason's wife, need concern us.   Mrs.
John has lost a baby, to her inconsolable sorrow.
During a long absence of her husband from home a
Polish servant girl gives birth to an illegitimate child,
whose father is Mrs. John's brutal brother, Bruno
Mechelke.   Bruno is not disposed to assume the re-

sponsibilities either of a father or of a husband.
Mrs. John assures the mother to be, that if the child is
given to the Johns it shall be cared for like a prince.
The child is born in a garret, and given over to Mrs.
John, who promptly writes to her husband that she
has borne him a child. Later the real mother seeks
to recover the child, and Mrs. John uses both force
and fraud to retain it. The true mother becomes
troublesome and Bruno brutally murders her. An in-
vestigation is made. Mrs. John is convicted of fraud
in connection with the child but protests her innocence
of any complicity in the murder. And she destroys
herself for grief and shame. It is a somber tragedy
of attics and dark alleys, the rat-frequented portion
of the world, powerfully expressing, however, the ca-
pacity for sin of a woman under the domination of
the maternal instinct.

In contrast to this we may set the powerful French
play *Madame X,* by Alexander Bisson, which illus-
trates the power of maternal love surviving in the
midst of degradation and shame. Madame Floriot
has deserted her husband and child. In a few years
her lover dies and she returns to her husband but he
drives her out of the house, refusing to let her even
look at her son. For twenty years she rolls in the
mire, and from bad to worse. Youth and beauty are
gone. She drowns her sorrows in absinthe and in
ether, and lives a wretched life with one man after an-
other. One day she returns from Buenos Ayres to
Bordeaux, in company with an adventurer named Le-
roque, a particularly despicable fellow. Leroque

meets with some of his former associates, and a plot is formed by which they hope to get possession of Madame Floriot's dower of 125,000 francs. This, under the French law, she had a right to claim, but she has left it with her husband and has endured twenty years of misery and privation in order that the money may revert to her son. Leroque, learning the situation, prepares to start for Paris, deaf alike to the entreaties and the commands of Madame Floriot. To thwart him, she shoots him, and quietly gives herself into custody.

In the trial her defense is assigned to her young son Raymond, now grown to manhood. While in prison she preserves an absolute silence, lest the revelation of her identity should bring disgrace upon her son. It is only in the court room that she discovers that the attorney for the defense is her son. Her great emotion at the discovery so moves the young man that his eloquence stirs the jury and she is acquitted. But absinthe, ether and misery have done their work. A few minutes after the trial, and just when Raymond has come to realize that it is his mother whom he has defended, she expires.

A play by an American author, Edwin Milton Royle, entitled *The Squaw Man* well deserves mention here. A young Englishman, generous to a fault, has settled in the cow-boy country. Here a little Indian princess falls in love with him. And after she has twice saved his life, once at imminent peril of her own, he marries her, although by so doing he loses caste with the white men who despise the " Squaw man " or husband of a squaw. The Englishman and his squaw have a little boy who has reached the age of four or five years when news comes from England that the father is heir to a noble title, and that the woman for whose love he left England is now a widow still young and beautiful, and waiting for him. He refuses to budge. He would not desert even a dog that had been so faithful to him as has his Indian wife. But he is finally persuaded to send his son to England to be educated for the high position that awaits him. The little squaw, however, cannot consent to be separated from her child, and kills herself when it is taken from her.

The Irish playwrights, whose work has recently delighted large audiences throughout the English-speaking world, have given us at least two plays centered upon motherhood: *The Riders to the Sea* by John M. Synge, and *The Gaol Gate* by Lady Gregory. Both are profoundly touching, largely because of the extraordinary beauty of the lines, which are like prose lyrics inspired by passionate feeling. *The Riders to the Sea* resembles some of Ibsen's work, especially *Rosmersholm* in the supernatural background, and various plays of Ibsen in the degree to which the dialogue reveals the past even while it carries the story to its end. A mother of the Arran Islands, on the west coast of Ireland, has lost her sons by shipwreck, one after another, until now Bartley, the last, is about to embark even while a storm is threatening and when supernatural omens of disaster are manifest. Bartley is deaf to prayer and entreaty and suffers the fate of his brothers. When he is brought home on a stretcher the keening of the mother rises to a solemn chant of magnificent power. In poetic beauty there has been no such play in our language since the great plays of Shakespeare. The almost bald simplicity of the plot is redeemed by numerous little touches that reveal the author's peculiar intimacy with the life of the Arran Islanders. Alike on the stage and in the closet the illusion of reality is powerfully sustained by this moving masterpiece. Especially brilliant, subtle and original is the note of triumph and consolation that blends with the mother's chant of sorrow. Even the present sorrow is less painful to her than the eternal fear and suspense which have been well nigh her whole portion as a mother of sea-faring sons. This is not unmaternal; and it is wonderfully human.

Lady Gregory's *The Gaol Gate* is a very short play. Two old women, one of them the mother, come to the jail before dawn, to hear the last words of a young man who is involved in a murder case. They have heard that he has informed against his associates. But after long waiting they hear that the young man is already dead, and has betrayed nobody. The peculiar horror in which the Irish peasants hold one who turns king's evidence is the underlying sentiment of the play. And the aged mother's keening is as a song of triumph that her son did not betray his associates. It has been my privilege to hear Lady Gregory herself read from this play, whose literary beauty she especially knows how to bring out.

Ibsen's *Ghosts* is a powerful play expressing not

only the dire effects of heredity, but also the long and terrible misery of a woman who lives with a dissipated husband, to find in the end that the life of her son is ruined by the dissipation of the father. *Maternity* by Brieux is a protest against the efforts of the French government to increase the population; a plea that motherhood is always sacred even when it is the result of crime; and a protest against a French law forbidding legal inquiry into the paternity of an illegitimate child. Adequately to discuss the propositions inculcated by this play would require a long space. The play contains much that is stimulating and thought-provoking, and exhibits considerable dramaturgic skill.

Of course, these examples do not exhaust the subject of the mother in drama. Yet it is true that plays specially illustrative of motherhood are singularly, and indeed unaccountably, scarce. And the field is nearly virgin soil for those who venture into it.

THE HAPPY HOUR

By MARY FRANCES BUTTS

The busy day is over,
The household work is done;
The cares that fret the morning
Have faded with the sun;
And in the tender twilight,
I sit in happy rest,
With my precious rosy baby
Asleep upon my breast.

White lids with silken fringes
Shut out the waning light;
A little hand close folded,
Holds mamma's fingers tight;
And in their soft white wrappings
At last in perfect rest,
Two dainty feet are cuddled,
Like birdies in a nest.

All hopes and loves unworthy
Fade out at this sweet hour;
All pure and noble longings
Renew their holy power;
For Christ, who in the Virgin
Our motherhood has blest,
Is near to every woman
With a baby on her breast.

EUGENE FIELD ON MOTHERHOOD

By Ida Comstock Below

While his love and thoughtfulness for children was one of his greatest charms, both in his life and writings, he did more to elevate motherhood than any other writer of the present day.

The women he admired most were not the devotees of fashion, nor even those of the higher literary attainments, unless they also best loved their own firesides and to rock the cradle. The mother-love is nowhere more beautifully portrayed than in the story of " Félice and Petit Poulain," where an old family horse is seized by the German soldiers while marching upon France, and driven many miles away; after a fierce battle, riderless and blood-stained she gallops over the country back to the little colt she left behind, only to find him dead amid the ruins of the farmyard. I quote from that story this little tribute to our animal friends:

" There are those who say that none but human-kind is immortal — that none but man has a soul. I do not make or believe that claim. There is that within me which tells me that nothing in this world and life of ours which has felt the grace of maternity shall utterly perish, and this I say in all reverence, and with the hope that I offend neither God nor man."

MOTHER'S LOVE

By Thomas Burbidge

He sang so wildly, did the Boy,
That you could never tell
If 'twas a madman's voice you heard,
Or if the spirit of a bird
Within his heart did dwell:
A bird that dallies with his voice
Among the matted branches;
Or on the free blue air his note
To pierce, and fall, and rise, and float,
With bolder utterance launches.
None ever was so sweet as he,

The boy that wildly sang to me;
Though toilsome was the way and long,
He led me not to lose the song.

But when again we stood below
The unhidden sky, his feet
Grew slacker, and his note more slow,
But more than doubly sweet.
He led me then a little way
Athwart the barren moor,
And then he stayed and bade me stay
Beside a cottage door;
I could have stayed of mine own will,
In truth, my eye and heart to fill
With the sweet sight which I saw there,
At the dwelling of the cottager.

A little in the doorway sitting,
The mother plied her busy knitting,
And her cheek so softly smiled,
You might be sure, although her gaze
Was on the meshes of the lace,
Yet her thoughts were with her child.
But when the boy had heard her voice,
As o'er her work she did rejoice,
His became silent altogether,
And slily creeping by the wall
He seiz'd a single plume, let fall
By some wild bird of longest feather;
And all a-tremble with his freak,
He touch'd her lightly on the cheek.

Oh, what a loveliness her eyes
Gather in that one moment's space,
While peeping round the post she spies
Her darling's laughing face!
Oh, mother's love is glorifying,
On the cheek like sunset lying;
In the eyes a moisten'd light,
Softer than the moon at night!

QUOTATIONS

Unhappy is the man for whom his own mother has not made all other mothers venerable.   RICHTER.

There is in all this cold and hollow world no fount of deep, strong, deathless love, save that within a mother's heart.   MRS. HEMANS.

A man never sees all that his mother has been to him till it's too late to let her know that he sees it.
W. D. HOWELLS.

If you would reform the world from its errors and vices, begin by enlisting the mothers. C. SIMMONS.

I think it must somewhere be written, that the virtues of the mothers shall be visited on their children, as well as the sins of the fathers. CHARLES DICKENS.

The mother's yearning, that completest type of life within another life which is the essence of human love, feels the presence of the cherished child, even in the base degraded man.   GEORGE ELIOT.

The dignity, the grandeur, the tenderness, the everlasting and divine significance of motherhood.

DE WITT TALLMADGE.

I would desire for a friend the son who never resisted the tears of his mother. LACRETELLE.

The babe first feeds upon the mother's bosom, but is always on her heart. H. W. BEECHER.

Say to mothers, what a holy charge is theirs, with what a kingly power their love might rule the fountains of the new-born mind. MRS. SIGOURNEY.

Oh, wondrous power! how little understood,
　　Entrusted to the mother's mind alone,
To fashion genius, form the soul for good,
　　Inspire a West, or train a Washington.

MRS. HALE.

What are Raphael's Madonnas but the shadow of a mother's love, fixed in permanent outline forever.

T. W. HIGGINSON.

No language can express the power and beauty and heroism and majesty of a mother's love. It shrinks not where man cowers, and grows stronger where man faints, and over the wastes of worldly fortune sends the radiance of quenchless fidelity like a star in heaven. E. H. CHAPIN.

A mother's love is indeed the golden link that binds youth to age; and he is still but a child, however time may have furrowed his cheek, or silvered his brow, who can yet recall, with softened heart, the fond devotion, or the gentle chidings, of the best friend that God ever gives us. BOVEE.

It is generally admitted, and very frequently proved, that virtue and genius, and all the natural good qualities which men possess, are derived from their mothers. HOOK.

An ounce of mother is worth a pound of clergy.

SPANISH PROVERB.

The mother's heart is the child's school-room.

H. W. BEECHER.

Children, look in those eyes, listen to that dear voice, notice the feeling of even a single touch that is bestowed upon you by that gentle hand! Make much of it while yet you have that most precious of all good gifts, a loving mother. Read the unfathomable love of those eyes; the kind anxiety of that tone and look, however slight your pain. In after life you may have friends, fond, dear friends, but never will you have again the inexpressible love and gentleness lavished upon you, which none but a mother can bestow. T. MACAULAY.

Men are what their mothers make them.

R. W. EMERSON.

The instruction received at the mother's knee, and the paternal lessons, together with the pious and sweet souvenirs of the fireside, are never entirely effaced from the soul. LAMENNAIS.

If the whole world were put into one scale, and my mother in the other, the whole world would kick the beam. LORD LANGDALE.

No joy in nature is so sublimely affecting as the joy of a mother at the good fortune of her child.

RICHTER.

The mother in her office holds the key of the soul; and she it is who stamps the coin of character, and makes the being who would be a savage but for her gentle cares, a Christian man! Then crown her queen of the world. OLD PLAY.

Observe how soon, and to what a degree, a mother's influence begins to operate! Her first ministration for her infant is to enter, as it were, the valley of the shadow of death, and win its life at the peril of her own! How different must an affection thus founded be from all others! MRS. SIGOURNEY.

A mother's love — how sweet the name!
What is a mother's love?
A noble, pure, and tender flame,
    Enkindled from above,
To bless a heart of earthly mold;
The warmest love that can grow cold: —
    This is a mother's love.

J. MONTGOMERY.

I worship thee, O Sun! whose ample light,
Blessing every forehead, ripening every fruit,
Entering every flower and every hovel,

Pours itself forth and yet is never less,
Still spending and unspent — like mother's love!

EDMOND ROSTAND.

Number thy lamps of love, and tell me, now,
How many canst thou relight at the stars
And blush not at their burning? One — one only —
Lit while your pulses by one heart kept time,
And fed with faithful fondness to your grave —
(Tho' sometimes with a hand stretch'd back from
    heaven),
Steadfast through all things — near, when most for-
    got
And with its fingers of unerring truth
Pointing the lost way in the darkest hour —
One lamp — thy mother's love — amid the stars
Shall lift its pure flame changeless, and before
The throne of God, burn through eternity —
Holy — as it was lit and lent thee here.

NATHANIEL P. WILLIS.

Oh! when a mother meets on high
The Babe she lost in infancy,
Hath she not then, for pains and fears,
The day of woe, the watchful night,
For all her sorrow, all her tears,
An over-payment of delight?

ROBERT SOUTHEY.

Earth held no symbol, had no living sign
To image forth the mother's deathless love.

MRS. HALE.

The love of a mother is never exhausted, it never changes, it never tires. A father may turn his back on his child, brothers and sisters become inveterate enemies, husbands may desert their wives, wives their husbands. But a mother's love endures through all; in good repute, in bad repute, in the face of the world's condemnation, a mother still loves on, and still hopes that her child may turn from his evil ways, and repent; still she remembers the infant smiles that once filled her bosom with rapture, the merry laugh, the joyful shout of his childhood, the opening promise of his youth; and she can never be brought to think him all unworthy.   WASHINGTON IRVING.

A mother's love!
If there be one thing pure,
Where all beside is sullied,
That can endure,
When all else passes away;
If there be aught
Surpassing human deed or word, or thought,
It is a mother's love.

MARCHIONESS DE SPADARA.

Poor George Somers had known what it was to be in sickness, and none to soothe — lonely and in prison, and none to visit him. He could not endure his mother from his sight; if she moved away, his eye would follow her. She would sit for hours by his bed, watching him as he slept. Sometimes he would start from a feverish dream, and look anxiously up until he saw her bending over him, when he would

take her hand, lay it on his bosom, and fall asleep with
the tranquillity of a child. In this way he died.

WASHINGTON IRVING.

TRANSFIGURATION

By LOUISA M. ALCOTT

On the death of her mother

Mysterious death! who in a single hour
    Life's gold can so refine,
    And by thy art divine
Change mortal weakness to immortal power!

Bending beneath the weight of eighty years,
    Spent with the noblest strife
    Of a victorious life,
We watched her fading heavenward, through our tears.

But ere the sense of loss our hearts had wrung,
    A miracle was wrought;
    And swift as happy thought
She lived again,— brave, beautiful, and young.

Age, pain, and sorrow dropped the veils they wore
    And showed the tender eyes
    Of angels in disguise,
Whose discipline so patiently she bore.

The past years brought their harvest rich and fair;
    While memory and love,
    Together, fondly wove
A golden garland for the silver hair.

How could we mourn like those who are bereft,
    When every pang of grief
    Found balm for its relief
In counting up the treasures she had left? —

Faith that withstood the shocks of toil and time;
    Hope that defied despair;
    Patience that conquered care;
And loyalty, whose courage was sublime;

The great deep heart that was a home for all, —
    Just, eloquent, and strong
    In protest against wrong;
Wide charity, that knew no sin, no fall;

The Spartan spirit that made life so grand,
    Mating poor daily needs
    With high, heroic deeds,
That wrested happiness from Fate's hard hand.

We thought to weep, but sing for joy instead,
    Full of the grateful peace
    That follows her release;
For nothing but the weary dust lies dead.

Oh, noble woman! never more a queen
    Than in the laying down
    Of scepter and of crown
To win a greater kingdom, yet unseen:

Teaching us how to seek the highest goal,
   To earn the true success, —
   To live, to love, to bless, —
And make death proud to take a royal soul.

THE MOTHER IN FICTION

By Stephen Williams

In the world of imaginative literature, as in actual
life, the mother is a supreme figure. All sorts of
women lend their enchantment to the pages of books,
from the unscrupulous Becky Sharp to the sweet, pure,
lovely heroines of *Waverley*. In the *Waverley Novels*
womanhood approaches perfection. Di Vernon and
the Jewess Rebecca are my favorite heroines in all
fiction. Scott's women, however, are mostly free
from exacting family obligations.

Jane Austen's characters and situations are always
interesting, but her mothers are the most contemptible
in English fiction. How we have wished that we could
free them from their mercenary matrimonial pur-
suits! There is scarcely any variety of types, but Mrs.
Bennett in *Pride and Prejudice* is the weakest and
most lacking in sense. Mrs. Dashwood in *Sense and
Sensibility*, and Lady Bertram in *Mansfield Park*,
are so lifelike that they appear as old acquaintances,
and will live as long as books are read. Few and
simple were the incidents of Miss Austen's brief life,
but she has described the society she knew with great

truth and simplicity. In passing to Anthony Trollope we have an abundance of material out of which it is not easy to choose. In Trollope's novels the interest is almost exclusively of a domestic nature, and we have some fine studies of the maternal relation. *The Small House at Allington* is one of his best stories, and the widow, Mrs. Dale, will always claim a warm place in our affections. Perhaps she made too many sacrifices for her daughters, but a true mother's heart knows no greater joy than comes from just these sacrifices. "Her own girls loved her, and respected her, and that was pretty much all that she demanded of the world on her behalf." Mrs. Crawley in *Framley Parsonage,* though only a secondary character, will always claim our sympathy. Life must have seemed very sordid to her as she thought of the wives of the neighboring clergy — Mrs. Proudie, Mrs. Arabin, Mrs. Grantly and Mrs. Mark Robarts. The good mother kept patiently on her way in spite of all privations,

> Darning little stockings for restless little feet,
> Washing little faces to keep them clean and sweet,
> Sewing on the buttons, overseeing rations,
> Soothing with a kind word others' lamentations.

Lady Lufton was a most devoted mother, sensible too, on the whole, but could not get rid of the notion that her son should marry a wife of her choosing. "The only thing quite certain to her was this, that life would not be worth living if she were forced into a permanent quarrel with her son." Mrs. Proudie plays her part in novel after novel, and is one of the most odious women in fiction.

Dickens's description of Mrs. Jellyby is a satire on literary women who neglect children and home. Mrs. Jellyby was the mother of a large family, but as devoid of the maternal spirit as though it had no existence in life. Of course the character is rather overdrawn, but exaggeration does not deface reality. There are Mrs. Jellybys to-day, as there were when *Bleak House* was written. The foolish mother constantly indulging and flattering her boy, blind to all his faults, is drawn for us in Mrs. Steerforth.

Bayard Taylor gives us a most touching and pathetic picture of true mother love in *John Godfrey's Fortunes*. We see the widow taking in sewing that she may educate her boy, and concealing from him the cancer that tortures her whole frame. To make provision for John's future was the one object of her life. For his sake she lived bravely and cheerfully, till the concealed malady laid her on the bed from which she never rose. Surely something more substantial than imagination accounted for Mrs. Godfrey! " At one time, I think, she would have willingly stopped the march of my years, and been content to keep me at her side, a boy forever. I was incapable of detecting this feeling at the time, and perhaps I wrong her memory in alluding to it now. God knows I have often wished it could have been so! Whatever of natural selfishness there may have been in the thought, she weighed it down, out of sight, by all those years of self-denial, and the final sacrifice, for my sake. No truer, tenderer, more simple-hearted mother ever lived than Barbara Godfrey."

In the *Scarlet Letter,* when they thought of taking the child away, Hawthorne gives us a masterly characterization of a mother's strong love turned almost to madness. We feel the throbbing of the mother's heart as she exclaims, " God gave her into my keeping. I will not give her up. . . . I will not lose the child."

There is a deep and beautiful tenderness in the tribute which St. Clare pays to his mother in *Uncle Tom's Cabin.* Mrs. Stowe says this expresses the influence their mother had left with them all. St. Clare's mother was the personification of all that is beautiful and good.

On the death of Mr. Barrie's mother and eldest sister, within three days of each other, it became known that they were the originals of Jess and Leeby in *A Window in Thrums.* " Leeby had taken Jess's hand — a worn old hand that had many a time gone out in love and kindness when younger hands were cold. Poets have sung and fighting men have done great deeds for hands that never had such a record." Robertson Nicoll tells us that Mrs. Barrie's happy, peaceful life knew one tragedy, and that Barrie drew his inspiration from this tragedy in his mother's life when he wrote the intensely pathetic chapter, " Dead This Twenty Years." Jess will always claim and hold the love of every one who cherishes the memory of a good mother.

In *East Lynne,* Mrs. Henry Wood shows us a mother's bleeding heart as no one else has done with equal pathos and completeness. The immense effect which Lady Isabel had upon my mind when I first read the book has continued through life. When she has the opportunity of going to the Carlyle's in the capacity of governess to her own children, the picture becomes almost intolerably pathetic. " She battled with herself that day; now resolving to go, and risk it; now shrinking from the attempt. At one moment it seemed to her that Providence must have placed this opportunity in her way that she might see her children in her desperate longing. . . . Evening came and she had not decided. She passed another night of pain, of restlessness, of longing for her children; this intense longing appeared to be overmastering all her powers of mind and body. The temptation at length proved too strong; the project, having been placed before her covetous eyes, could not be relinquished, and she finally resolved to go. 'What is it that should keep me away?' she argued. 'The dread of discovery? Well, if that comes it must. . . . Deeper humiliation than ever would be my portion, when they drive me from East Lynne with abhorrence and ignominy, as a soldier is drummed out of his regiment; but I could bear that, as I must bear the rest, and I can shrink under some hedge and lay myself down to die. Humiliation for me! No; I will not put that in comparison with seeing and living with my children.'" There is something characteristically maternal in Mrs. Hare's deep and tender love for poor Richard. " Fretting after that vagabond," the stern old Justice called it.

Though we might prolong our list almost indefinitely we may safely say that, as the office of mother is the most sacred upon earth, the literature of motherhood is the one certain field in which the best is yet to be said.

THE MOTHER'S HYMN

By William Cullen Bryant *

"Blessed art thou among women"

Lord who ordainest for mankind
    Benignant toils and tender cares,
We thank thee for the ties that bind
    The mother to the child she bears.

We thank Thee for the hopes that rise
    Within her heart, as, day by day,
The dawning soul, from those young eyes,
    Looks with a clearer, steadier ray.

And grateful for the blessing given
    With that dear infant on her knee,
She trains the eye to look to heaven,
    The voice to lisp a prayer to Thee.

Such thanks the blessed Mary gave
    When from her lap the Holy Child,
Sent from on high to seek and save
    The lost of earth, looked up and smiled.

All-Gracious! grant to those who bear
    A mother's charge, the strength and light
To guide the feet that own their care
    In ways of Love and Truth and Right.

* *From the " Bryant Anthology."   Ford, Howard, Hulbert.*

III

CHILD TO MOTHER

VALENTINES TO MY MOTHER

By Christina G. Rossetti *

1876

Fairer than younger beauties, more beloved
    Than many a wife,
By stress of Time's vicissitudes unmoved
    From settled calm of life;

Endearing rectitude to those who watch
    The verdict of your face,
Raising and making gracious those who catch
    A semblance of your grace:

With kindly lips of welcome, and with pleased
    Propitious eyes benign,
Accept a kiss of homage from your least
    Last Valentine.

1877

Own Mother dear,
We all rejoicing here
Wait for each other,
Daughter for Mother,
Sister for Brother,
Till each dear face appear

Transfigured by Love's flame
Yet still the same,—
The same yet new,—
My face to you,
Your face to me,
Made lovelier by Love's flame
But still the same;
Most dear to see
In halo of Love's flame,
Because the same.

1878

Blessed Dear and Heart's Delight,
Companion, Friend and Mother mine,
Round whom my fears and love entwine,—
With whom I hope to stand and sing
Where Angels form the outer ring
Round singing Saints, who clad in white,
Know no more of day or night
Or death or any changeful thing,
Or anything that is not love,
Human love and Love Divine,—
Bid me to that tryst above,
Bless your Valentine.

1879

Mother mine,
Whom every year
Doth endear,—
Before sweet Spring

(That sweetest thing
Brimful of bliss)
  Sets all the throng
    Of birds a-wooing,
    Billing and cooing,—
Your Valentine
  Sings you a song,
Gives you a kiss.

1880

More shower than shine
Brings sweet St. Valentine;
Warm shine, warm shower,
Bring up sweet flower on flower.
Through shower and shine
Loves you your Valentine,
Through shine, through shower,
Through summer's flush, through autumn's fading
    hour.

1881

Too cold almost for hope of Spring
  Or first fruits from the realm of flowers,
Your dauntless Valentine, I bring
One sprig of love, and sing
  " Love has no Winter hours."

If even in this world love is love
  (This wintry world which felt the Fall),
What must it be in heaven above

Where love to great and small
Is all in all?

1882

My blessed Mother dozing in her chair
    On Christmas Day seemed an embodied Love,
A comfortable Love with soft brown hair
    Softened and silvered to a tint of dove;
A better sort of Venus with an air
    Angelical from thoughts that dwell above;
A wiser Pallas in whose body fair
    Enshrined a blessed soul looks out thereof.
Winter brought holly then; now Spring has brought
    Paler and frailer snowdrops shivering;
And I have brought a simple humble thought —
    I her devoted duteous Valentine —
A lifelong thought which thrills this song I sing,
    A lifelong love to this dear Saint of mine.

1883

A world of change and loss, a world of death,
Of heart and eyes that fail, of laboring breath,
Of pains to bear and painful deeds to do: —
Nevertheless a world of life to come
And love; where you're at home, while in our home
Your Valentine rejoices, having you.

1884

Another year of joy and grief,
    Another year of hope and fear:

O Mother, is life long or brief?
  We hasten while we linger here.

But, since we linger, love me still
  And bless me still, O Mother mine,
While hand in hand we scale life's hill,
  You guide, and I your Valentine.

1885

All the Robin Redbreasts
  Have lived the winter through,
Jenny Wrens have pecked their fill
  And found a work to do;
Families of Sparrows
  Have weathered wind and storm
With Rabbit on the stony hill
  And Hare upon her form.

You and I, my Mother,
  Have lived the winter through,
And still we play our daily parts
  And still find work to do;
And still the cornfields flourish,
  The olive and the vine,
And still you reign my Queen of Hearts
  And I'm your Valentine.

1886

Winter's latest snowflake is the snowdrop flower,
  Yellow crocus kindles the first flame of the Spring,

At the time appointed, at that day and hour,
   When life reawakens and hope in everything.

Such a tender snowflake in the wintry weather,
   Such a feeble flamelet for chilled St. Valentine,—
But blest be any weather which finds us still together,
   My pleasure and my treasure, O blessed Mother
      mine.

   * By permission of The Macmillan Company.

CHILD AND MOTHER

By Eugene Field *

O Mother-my-Love, if you'll give me your hand,
   And go where I ask you to wander,
I will lead you away to a beautiful land —
   The Dreamland that's waiting out yonder.
We'll walk in a sweet-posie garden out there
   Where moonlight and starlight are streaming
And the flowers and birds are filling the air
   With fragrance and music of dreaming.

There'll be no little tired-out boy to undress,
   No questions or cares to perplex you;
There'll be no little bruises or bumps to caress,
   Nor patching of stockings to vex you.
For I'll rock you away on a silver-dew stream,
   And sing you asleep when you're weary,
And no one shall know of our beautiful dream
   But you and your own little dearie.

And when I am tired I'll nestle my head
  In the bosom that's soothed me so often,
And the wide-awake stars shall sing in my stead
  A song which our dreaming shall soften.
So Mother-my-Love, let me take your dear hand,
  And away through the starlight we'll wander —
Away through the mist to the beautiful land —
  The Dreamland that's waiting out yonder!

By courtesy of Charles Scribner's Sons.

THE MERCHANT

By Rabindranath Tagore *

Imagine, mother, that you are to stay at home and I to travel into strange lands.

Imagine that my boat is ready at the landing, fully laden.

Now think well, mother, before you say what I shall bring for you when I come back.

Mother, do you want heaps of gold?

There by the banks of golden streams, fields are full of golden harvest.

And in the shade of the forest path the golden *champa* flowers drop on the ground.

I will gather them all for you in many hundred baskets.

Mother do you want pearls as big as the rain-drops of autumn?

I shall cross to the pearl island shore.

There in the early morning light pearls tremble on the meadow flowers, pearls drop on the grass, and pearls are scattered on the sand by the wild sea-waves.

My brother shall have a pair of horses with wings to fly among the clouds.

For my father I shall bring a magic pen that, without his knowing, will write of itself.

For you, mother, I must have the casket and jewel that cost seven kings their kingdoms.

THE END

By Rabindranath Tagore *

It is time for me to go, mother; I am going.

When in the paling darkness of the lonely dawn you stretch out your arms for your baby in the bed, I shall say " Baby is not there! "— mother I am going.

I shall become a delicate draught of air and caress you; and I shall be ripples in the water when you bathe, and kiss you, and kiss you again.

In the gusty night when the rain patters on the leaves you will hear my whisper in your bed, and my laughter will flash with the lightning through the open window into your room.

If you lie awake, thinking of your baby till late into the night, I shall sing to you from the stars, " Sleep, mother, sleep."

On the straying moonbeams I shall steal over your bed, and lie upon your bosom while you sleep.

I shall become a dream, and through the little opening of your eyelids I shall slip into the depths of your sleep, and when you wake up and look round startled, like a twinkling firefly I shall flit out into the darkness.

When, on the great festival of *puja,* the neighbors' children come and play about the house, I shall melt into the music of the flute and throb in your heart all day.

Dear Auntie will come with *puja*-presents and will ask, " Where is our baby, sister? " Mother, you will tell her softly, " He is in the pupils of my eyes, he is in my body and in my soul."

MY MOTHER'S GRAVE
ANONYMOUS

It was thirteen years since my mother's death, when after a long absence from my native village, I stood beside the sacred mound beneath which I had seen her buried. Since that mournful period, a great change had come over me. My childish years had passed away, and with them my youthful character. The world was altered too; and as I stood at my mother's grave, I could hardly realize that I was the same thoughtless, happy creature, whose cheeks she so often kissed in an excess of tenderness. But the varied events of thirteen years had not effaced the memory of that mother's smile. It seemed as if I had seen her but yesterday — as if the blessed sound of her well remembered voice was in my ear. The gay dreams of my infancy and childhood were brought back so distinctly to my mind, that had it not been for one bitter recollection, the tears I shed would have been gentle and refreshing. The circumstance may seem a trifling one — but the thought of it now pains my heart, and I relate it that those children who have parents to love them, may learn to value them as they ought.

My mother had been ill a long time, and I had become so accustomed to her pale face and weak voice, that I was not frightened at them, as children usually are. At first, it is true, I sobbed violently; but when day after day, I returned from school, and found her the same, I began to believe she would always be spared to me; but they told me she would die.

One day when I had lost my place in the class, and done my work wrong side outward, I came home discouraged and fretful; — I went to my mother's chamber. She was paler than usual, but met me with the same affectionate smile that always welcomed my return. Alas! when I look back through the lapse of thirteen years, I think my heart must have been stone, not to have melted by it. She requested me to go down stairs, and bring her a glass of water; — I pettishly asked why she did not call a domestic to do it. With a look of mild reproach which I shall never forget if I live to be a hundred years old, she said, "And will not my daughter bring a glass of water for her poor sick mother?"

I went and brought her the water, but I did not do it kindly. Instead of smiling and kissing her, as I was wont to do, I set the glass down very quickly and left the room. After playing a short time, I went to bed without bidding my mother good night; but when alone in my room, in the darkness and the silence,

I remembered how pale she looked, and how her voice trembled when she said, " Will not my daughter bring a glass of water for her poor sick mother ! " I couldn't sleep. I stole into her chamber to ask forgiveness. She had sunk into an easy slumber, and they told me I must not waken her. I did not tell any one what troubled me, but stole back to bed, resolved to rise early in the morning, and tell her how sorry I was for my conduct.

The sun was shining brightly when I awoke, and hurrying on my clothes, I hastened to my mother's chamber. She was dead! she never spoke more — never smiled upon me again — and when I touched the hand that used to rest upon my head in blessing, it was so cold that it made me start. I bowed down by her side, and sobbed in the bitterness of my heart. I thought then I wished I might die, and be buried with her; and old as I now am, I would give worlds were they mine to give, could my mother but have lived to tell me she forgave my childish ingratitude. But I cannot call her back; and when I stand by her grave, and whenever I think of her manifold kindness, the memory of that reproachful look she gave me, will bite like a serpent, and sting like an adder.

TO MY MOTHER

By Henry Kirke White

And canst thou, Mother, for a moment think,
   That we, thy children, when old age shall shed
   Its blanching honors on thy weary head,

Could from our best of duties ever shrink?
Sooner the sun from his high sphere should sink
  Than we, ungrateful leave thee in that day,
  To pine in solitude thy life away,
Or shun thee, tottering on the grave's cold brink.
Banish the thought! — where'er our steps may roam,
  O'er smiling plains, or wastes without a tree,
  Still will fond memory point our hearts to thee,
And paint the pleasures of thy peaceful home;
While duty bids us all thy griefs assuage,
And smooth the pillow of thy sinking age.

MOTHERLESS

By Elizabeth Barrett Browning

I write.   My mother was a Florentine,
Whose rare blue eyes were shut from seeing me
When scarcely I was four years old; my life,
A poor spark snatched up from a failing lamp
Which went out therefore.   She was weak and frail;
She could not bear the joy of giving life —
The mother's rapture slew her.   If her kiss
Had left a longer weight upon my lips,
It might have steadied the uneasy breath,
And reconciled and fraternized my soul
With a new order.   As it was, indeed,
I felt a mother-want about the world,
And still went seeking, like a bleating lamb
Left out at night, in shutting up the fold, —
As restless as a nest-deserted bird

Grown chill through something being away, though
    what
It knows not. I, Aurora Leigh, was born
To make my father sadder, and myself
Not overjoyous, truly. Women know
The way to rear up children (to be just)
They know a simple, merry, tender knack
Of tying sashes, fitting baby-shoes,
And stringing pretty words that make no sense,
And kissing full sense into empty words;
Which things are corals to cut life upon,
Although such trifles: children learn by such
Love's holy earnest in a pretty play,
And get not over-early solemnized,—
But seeing, as in a rose-bush, Love's Divine,
Which burns and hurts not,— not a single bloom,—
Become aware and unafraid of Love.
Such good do mothers. Fathers love as well
— Mine did, I know,— but still with heavier brains,
And wills more consciously responsible,
And not as wisely, since less foolishly;
So mothers have God's license to be missed.

DEDICATIONS

THE QUEST   Edward Salisbury Field, 1904

To My Mother

    I've gone about for years I find
    With eyes half blind,
    Squandering golden hours

In search of flow'rs
That do not grow, it seems,
Except in dreams;
But in my wanderings
From place to place
I've found more fair no face —
No eyes more true than thine,
Oh mother mine.

THE LIGHT THAT FAILED By Rudyard Kipling *

If I were hanged on the highest hill,
Mother o'mine, O mother o'mine!
I know whose love would follow me still,
Mother o'mine, O mother o'mine!

If I were drowned in the deepest sea,
Mother o'mine, O mother o'mine!
I know whose tears would come down to me,
Mother o'mine, O mother o'mine!

If I were damned of body and soul,
Mother o'mine, O mother o'mine!
I know whose prayers would make me whole,
Mother o'mine, O mother o'mine!

* Copyright by Doubleday, Page & Company.

LYRICS OF EARTH By Archibald Lampman

Mother to whose valiant will,
Battling long ago,
What the heaping years fulfil,
Light and song, I owe,

Send my little book a-field,
Fronting praise or blame,
With the shining flag to shield
Of your name.

MOTHER By Kathleen Norris, 1911

As years ago we carried to your knees
The tales and treasures of eventful days,
Knowing no deed too humble for your praise,
Nor any gift too trivial to please,
So still we bring, with older smiles and tears,
What gifts we may, to claim the old, dear right;
Your faith, beyond the silence and the night,
Your love still close and watching through the years.

OVERHEARD IN ARCADY By Robert Bridges (Droch)*

Long years you've kept the door ajar
To greet me, coming from afar:
Long years in my accustomed place
I've read my welcome in your face,
And felt the sunlight of your love
Drive back the years and gently move
The telltale shadow 'round to youth,
You've found the very spring, in truth,
That baffles time — the kindly joy
That keeps me in your heart a boy.
And now I send an unknown guest
To bide with you and snugly rest
Beside the old home's ingle-nook.—
For love of me you'll love my book.

* By courtesy of the author from " Overheard in Arcady."

A SECULAR ODE ON THE NINTH JUBILEE OF ETON COLLEGE FOUNDER'S DAY

By Robert Bridges

Christ and his Mother, heavenly maid,
Mary, in whose fair name was laid
Eton's corner, bless our youth
With truth, and purity, mother of truth!

THE GARDEN MUSE

By William Aspenwall Bradley, 1910

To My Mother, a True Gardener

To you who've lived your life elate
In Marvell's happy garden state,
And doubtless see, with Milton's eyes,
Eden a flow'ry Paradise,
While every walk that you have trod,
Was Enoch's walk, a walk with God —
— To you this little book I bring
Wherein our English poets sing
Of all the pleasures they have found
In gardens grayly walled around,
Of tranquil toil and studious ease,
Mid flowers, shrubberies and trees,
Because you Cowley's wish have known
To have a garden of your own,
And having it, have plied that art
Which Temple calls the ladies' part,
So well, your skill might seem to be

A kind of gentle wizardry,
As still your flowers statelier grow
And with a richer color glow
Each summer, and perfume the air
More sweetly from each gay parterre.

    Ah, I recall the city plot
That was your scanty garden spot
In other years, and yet your care
Made e'en those narrow beds to bear
The narrower flinty walks between,
Such wealth of red and white and green
That prouder gardens might have sighed,
Grown pale through envy, and so, died.

    But now you hold your gentle sway
O'er a domain as broad as they,
Where you may tend with tranquil mind
The seeds and shoots and bulbs consigned
Each season to the garden soil,
Till, reared by you with patient toil,
At length in flaunting rows they stand
And keep the order you have planned,
The low before, the tall behind,
Their colors mingled and combined,
Gay household troops in order drawn
As for review upon the lawn,
While you the colonel seem to me
Of summer's splendid soldiery.

    Each morn I see you as you pass
Before them o'er the dewy grass,
Their files inspecting, while your eye
Scans all with sharpest scrutiny.

For you in all else mild, are yet
In this one thing a martinet.
And woe to that gay grenadier
Whose cap of crimson shall appear
One shade less bright,— however tall,
His head into your ark must fall.
Not Prussian Frederick did school
His soldiers with such iron rule.

    And yet they love you; see, how mute,
They greet you with a loud salute.
From every slender trump and bell
A martial music seems to swell,
Which, though 'tis lost to our dull ear.
I think your finer sense doth hear,
For you with music pass such hours
As are not given to your flow'rs,
Till blossoms spring among the keys,
And garden beds are symphonies.

THE PAGEANT AND OTHER POEMS

By Christina G. Rossetti, 1899

Sonnets are full of love, and this my tome
  Has many sonnets: so here now shall be
  One sonnet more, a love sonnet, from me
To her whose heart is my heart's quiet home,
  To my first Love, my Mother, on whose knee
I learnt love-lore that is not troublesome;
  Whose service is my special dignity,
And she my lodestar while I go and come.

And so because you love me, and because
   I love you, Mother, I have woven a wreath
      Of rhymes wherewith to crown your honored
         name:
   In you not fourscore years can dim the flame
Of love, whose blessed glow transcends the laws
   Of time and change and mortal life and death.

IN PRAISE OF LEAVES

By Lilian Shuman Dreyfus, 1906

To My Mother, Hettie Lang Shuman

Stumbling, we see the future as a cup
Which she no longer stores with bread and wine,
And where our human longing, yours and mine,
Is all the incense we may offer up.

A MOTHER'S PICTURE

By Edmund Clarence Stedman

She seemed an angel to our infant eyes!
Once, when the glorifying moon revealed
Her who at evening by our pillow kneeled —
Soft-voiced and golden-haired, from holy skies
Flown to her loves on wings of Paradise —
We looked to see the pinions half-concealed.
The Tuscan vines and olives will not yield
Her back to me, who loved her in this wise,
And since have little known her, but have grown
To see another mother, tenderly,

Watch over sleeping darlings of her own;
Perchance the years have changed her: yet alone
This picture lingers: still she seems to me
The fair, young Angel of my infancy.

TO MY MOTHER

By Thomas Moore

They tell us of an Indian tree
   Which howsoe'er the sun and sky
May tempt its boughs to wander free,
   And shoot and blossom, wide and high,
Far better loves to bend its arms
   Downward again to that dear earth
From which the life, that fills and warms
   Its grateful being, first had birth.
'Tis thus, though wooed by flattering friends,
   And fed with fame (if fame it be),
This heart, my own dear mother, bends,
   With love's true instinct, back to thee!

BEFORE IT IS TOO LATE

By George Bancroft Griffith

If you have a gray-haired mother
   In the old home far away,
Sit you down and write the letter
   You put off from day to day.

CHILD TO MOTHER

Don't wait until her weary steps
    Reach Heaven's pearly gate,
But show her that you think of her,
    Before it is too late.

If you have a tender message,
    Or a loving word to say,
Don't wait till you forget it,
    But whisper it to-day.
Who knows what bitter memories
    May haunt you if you wait?
So make your loved one happy
    Before it is too late.

The tender word unspoken,
    The letters never sent,
The long forgotten messages,
    The wealth of love unspent;
For these some hearts are breaking,
    For these some loved ones wait;
Show them that you care for them
    Before it is too late.

MY MOTHER

By Jane Taylor

Who fed me from her gentle breast,
And hushed me in her arms to rest,
And on my cheek sweet kisses pressed?
                My Mother.

When sleep forsook my open eye,
Who was it sang sweet lullaby,
And rocked me that I should not cry?
                              My Mother.

Who sat and watched my infant head,
When sleeping on my cradle bed,
And tears of sweet affection shed?
                              My Mother.

When pain and sickness made me cry,
Who gazed upon my heavy eye,
And wept for fear that I should die?
                              My Mother.

Who dressed my doll in clothes so gay,
And taught me pretty how to play,
And minded all I had to say?
                              My Mother.

Who ran to help me when I fell,
And would some pretty story tell,
Or kiss the place to make it well?
                              My Mother.

Who taught my infant lips to pray,
And love God's holy book and day,
And walk in wisdom's pleasant way?
                              My Mother.

And can I ever cease to be,
Affectionate and kind to thee,
Who was so very kind to me?

My Mother.

Ah! no, the thought I cannot bear,
And if God please my life to spare,
I hope I shall reward thy care,

My Mother.

When thou art feeble, old, and gray,
My healthy arms shall be thy stay,
And I will soothe thy pains away,

My Mother.

And when I see thee hang thy head,
'Twill be my turn to watch thy bed,
And tears of sweet affection shed,

My Mother.

For God, who lives above the skies,
Would look with vengeance in his eyes,
If I should ever dare despise

My Mother.

HALF-WAKING

By William Allingham *

I thought it was the little bed
I slept in long ago;

A straight white curtain at the head,
　And two smooth knobs below.

I thought I saw the nursery fire,
　And in a chair well-known
My mother sat, and did not tire
　With reading all alone.

If I should make the slightest sound
　To show that I'm awake,
She'd rise, and lap the blankets round,
　My pillow softly shake;

Kiss me and turn my face to see
　The shadows on the wall,
And then sing " Rousseau's Dream " to me
　Till fast asleep I fall.

But this is not my little bed;
　That time is far away:
With strangers now I live instead,
　From dreary day to day.

From " The Victorian Anthology," published by Houghton Mifflin Company.

TO A CHILD EMBRACING HIS MOTHER

BY THOMAS HOOD

Love thy mother, little one!
　Kiss and clasp her neck again —
Hereafter she may have a son
　Will kiss and clasp her neck in vain.
Love thy mother, little one!

Gaze upon her living eyes,
  And mirror back her love for thee,—
Hereafter thou mayst shudder sighs
  To meet them when they cannot see.
Gaze upon her living eyes!

Press her lips the while they glow
  With love that they have often told,—
Hereafter thou mayst press in woe,
  And kiss them till thine own are cold.
Press her lips the while they glow!

Oh, revere her raven hair!
  Although it be not silver-gray —
Too early Death, led on by Care,
  May snatch save one dear lock away.
Oh, revere her raven hair!

Pray for her at eve and morn,
  That Heaven may long the stroke defer;—
For thou mayst live the hour forlorn
  When thou wilt ask to die with her.
Pray for her at eve and morn!

TO MY MOTHER
By Robert Haven Schauffler

I see your face as on that calmer day
When from my infant eyes it passed away
  Beyond these petty cares and questionings
  Beyond this sphere of sordid human things —
The trampled field of time's capricious play.

Bright with more mother-love than tongue can say,
Stern with the sense of foes in strong array,
    Yet hopeful, with no hopefulness earth brings —
      I see your face.

O gracious guarder from the primrose way,
O loving guide when wayward feet would stray,
    O inspiration sweet when the heart sings,
    O patient ministrant to sufferings,
Down the long road, *madonna mia,* may
      I see your face.

MY MOTHER'S BIBLE

By George Pope Morris

This book is all that's left me now,—
    Tears will unbidden start,—
With faltering lip and throbbing brow
    I press it to my heart.
For many generations past
    Here is our family tree;
My mother's hands this Bible clasped,
    She, dying, gave it me.

Ah! well do I remember those
    Whose names these records bear;
Who round the hearthstone used to close,
    After the evening prayer,
And speak of what these pages said
    In tones my heart would thrill!

Though they are with the silent dead,
  Here are they living still!

My father read this holy book
  To brothers, sisters, dear;
How calm was my poor mother's look,
  Who loved God's word to hear!
Her angel face,— I see it yet!
  What thronging memories come!
Again that little group is met
  Within the halls of home!

Thou truest friend man ever knew,
  Thy constancy I've tried;
When all were false, I found thee true,
  My counselor and guide.
The mines of earth no treasures give
  That could this volume buy;
In teaching me the way to live,
  It taught me how to die!

THE DEAR OLD TOILING ONE

By David Gray *

Oh, many a leaf will fall to-night
As she wanders through the wood!
And many an angry gust will break
The dreary solitude.
I wonder if she's past the bridge,
Where Luggie moans beneath,

While rain-drops clash in planted lines
On rivulet and heath.
Disease hath laid his palsied palm
Upon my aching brow;
The headlong blood of twenty-one
Is thin and sluggish now.
'Tis nearly ten! A fearful night,
Without a single star
To light the shadow on her soul
With sparkle from afar:
The moon is canopied with clouds,
And her burden it is sore;
What would poor Jackie do, if he
Should never see her more?
Aye, light the lamp, and hang it up
At the window fair and free;
'Twill be a beacon on the hill
To let your mother see.
And trim it well, my little Ann,
For the night is wet and cold,
And you know the weary, winding way
Across the miry wold.
All drench'd will be her simple gown,
And the wet will reach her skin:
I wish that I could wander down,
And the red quarry win,
To take the burden from her back,
And place it upon mine;
With words of cheerful condolence,
Not utter'd to repine.
You have a kindly mother, dears,

As ever bore a child,
And Heaven knows I love her well
In passion undefil'd.
Ah me! I never thought that she
Would brave a night like this,
While I sit weaving by the fire
A web of fantasies.
How the winds beat this home of ours
With arrow-falls of rain;
This lonely home upon the hill
They beat with might and main.
And 'mid the tempest one lone heart
Anticipates the glow,
Whence, all her weary journey done,
Shall happy welcome flow.
'Tis after ten! O, were she here,
Young man although I be,
I could fall down upon her neck,
And weep right gushingly!
I have not lov'd her half enough,
The dear old toiling one,
The silent watcher by my bed,
In shadow or in sun.

From " The Victorian Anthology," published by Houghton Mifflin Company.

BOYHOOD

By Washington Allston

Ah, then how sweetly closed those crowded days!
The minutes parting one by one, like rays
 That fade upon a summer's eve.

But O, what charm or magic numbers
Can give me back the gentle slumbers
   Those weary, happy days did leave?
When by my bed I saw my mother kneel,
   And with her blessing took her nightly kiss;
   Whatever time destroys, he cannot this; —
E'en now that nameless kiss I feel.

SONGS FOR MY MOTHER *

By Anna Hempstead Branch

I

HER HANDS

My mother's hands are cool and fair,
   They can do anything.
Delicate mercies hide them there
   Like flowers in the spring.

When I was small and could not sleep,
   She used to come to me,
And with my cheek upon her hand
   How sure my rest would be.

For everything she ever touched
   Of beautiful or fine,
Their memories living in her hands
   Would warm that sleep of mine.

Her hands remember how they played
   One time in meadow streams, —

And all the flickering song and shade
  Of water took my dreams.

Swift through her haunted fingers pass
  Memories of garden things;—
I dipped my face in flowers and grass
  And sounds of hidden wings.

One time she touched the cloud that kissed
  Brown pastures bleak and far; —
I leaned my cheek into a mist
  And thought I was a star.

All this was very long ago
  And I am grown; but yet
The hand that lured my slumber so
  I never can forget.

For still when drowsiness comes on
  It seems so soft and cool,
Shaped happily beneath my cheek,
  Hollow and beautiful.

II

HER WORDS

My mother has the prettiest tricks
  Of words and words and words.
Her talk comes out as smooth and sleek
  As breasts of singing birds.

She shapes her speech all silver fine
  Because she loves it so.
And her own eyes begin to shine
  To hear her stories grow.

And if she goes to make a call
  Or out to take a walk
We leave our work when she returns
  And run to hear her talk.

We had not dreamed these things were so
  Of sorrow and of mirth.
Her speech is as a thousand eyes
  Through which we see the earth.

God wove a web of loveliness,
  Of clouds and stars and birds,
But made not anything at all
  So beautiful as words.

They shine around our simple earth
  With golden shadowings,
And every common thing they touch
  Is exquisite with wings.

There's nothing poor and nothing small
  But is made fair with them.
They are the hands of living faith
  That touch the garment's hem.

They are as fair as bloom or air,
   They shine like any star,
And I am rich who learned from her
   How beautiful they are.

* From " The Little Book of Modern Verse," by courtesy of the author.

MOTHER *

By Theresa Helburn

I have praised many loved ones in my song,
   And yet I stand
Before her shrine, to whom all things belong,
   With empty hand.

Perhaps the ripening future holds a time
   For things unsaid;
Not now; men do not celebrate in rhyme
   Their daily bread.

* From " The Little Book of Modern Verse," by courtesy of the author.

IT IS NOT YOURS, O MOTHER, TO COMPLAIN *

By Robert Louis Stevenson

It is not yours, O mother, to complain,
   Not, mother, yours to weep,
Though nevermore your son again
   Shall to your bosom creep,
      Though nevermore again you watch your
        baby sleep.

Though in the greener paths of earth,
  Mother and child, no more
We wander; and no more the birth
  Of me, whom once you bore,
  Seems still the brave reward that once it
    seemed of yore;

Though as all passes, day and night,
  The seasons and the years,
From you, O mother, this delight,
  This also disappears —
  Some profit yet survives of all your pangs
    and tears.

The child, the seed, the grain of corn,
  The acorn on the hill,
Each for some separate end is born
  In season fit, and still
  Each must in strength arise to work the al-
    mighty will.

So from the hearth the children flee,
  By that almighty hand
Austerely led: so one by sea
  Goes forth, and one by land:
  Nor aught of all man's sons escapes from that
    command.

So from the sally each obeys
  The unseen almighty nod;

So till the ending all their ways
    Blindfolded both have trod:
    Nor knew their task at all, but were the tools
        of God.

And as the fervent smith of yore
    Beat out the glowing blade,
Nor wielded in the front of war
    The weapons that he made,
    But in the tower at home still plied his ring-
        ing trade;

So like a sword the son shall roam
    On nobler missions sent;
And as the smith remained at home
    In peaceful turret pent,
    So sits the while at home the mother well
        content.

* *By permission of Charles Scribner's Sons.*

TO MY MOTHER

By Felicia Hemans

If e'er for human bliss or woe
I feel the sympathetic glow;
If e'er my heart has learn'd to know
    The gen'rous wish or prayer;
Who sow'd the germ with tender hand?
Who mark'd its infant leaves expand?
    My mother's fostering care.

And if one flower of charms refined
May grace the garden of my mind;
  'Twas she who nursed it there:
She loved to cherish and adorn
  Each blossom of the soil;
To banish every weed and thorn,
  That oft opposed her toil!

And oh! if e'er I sigh'd to claim,
The palm, the living palm of Fame,
  The glowing wreath of praise;
If e'er I wish'd the glittering stores,
That Fortune on her fav'rite pours;
'Twas but that wealth and fame, if mine,
Round Thee, with streaming rays might shine,
  And gild thy sun-bright days!

Yet not that splendor, pomp or power,
Might then irradiate every hour;
For these, my mother! well I know,
On thee no raptures could bestow;
But could thy bounty, warm and kind,
Be, like thy wishes, unconfined;
And fall as manna from the skies,
And bid a train of blessings rise,
  Diffusing joy and peace;
The tear-drop, grateful, pure, and bright,
For thee would beam with softer light,
Than all the diamond's crystal rays,
Than all the emerald's lucid blaze;

And joys of heaven would thrill thy heart,
To bid one bosom-grief depart,
    One tear, one sorrow cease!

Then, oh! may Heaven, that loves to bless,
Bestow the power to cheer distress;
Make thee its minister below,
To light the cloudy path of woe;
To visit the deserted cell,
Where indigence is doom'd to dwell;
To raise, when drooping to the earth,
The blossoms of neglected worth;
And round, with liberal hand, dispense
The sunshine of beneficence!

But ah! if Fate should still deny
Delights like these, too rich and high;
If grief and pain thy steps assail,
In life's remote and wintry vale:
Then as the wild Æolian lyre,
    Complains with soft entrancing number,
When the lone storm awakes the wire,
    And bids enchantment cease to slumber;
So filial love, with soothing voice,
E'en then shall teach thee to rejoice;
E'en then shall sweeter, milder sound,
When sorrow's tempest raves around;
While dark misfortune's gales destroy,
The frail mimosa-buds of hope and joy!

HOMESICK

By David Gray

Come to me, O my Mother! come to me,
Thine own son slowly dying far away!
Through the moist ways of the wide ocean, blown
By great invisible winds, come stately ships
To this calm bay for quiet anchorage;
They come, they rest awhile, they go away,
But, O my Mother, never comest thou!
The snow is round thy dwelling, the white snow,
That cold soft revelation pure as light,
And the pine-spire is mystically fringed,
Laced with incrusted silver. Here — ah me! —
The winter is decrepit, underborn,
A leper with no power but his disease.
Why am I from thee, Mother, far from thee?
Far from the frost enchantment, and the woods
Jewelled from bough to bough?   O home, my home!
O river in the valley of my home,
With mazy-winding motion intricate,
Twisting thy deathless music underneath
The polished ice-work,— must I nevermore
Behold thee with familiar eyes, and watch
Thy beauty changing with the changeful day,
Thy beauty constant to the constant change?

HYMN OF A VIRGIN OF DELPHI AT THE TOMB OF HER MOTHER

By Thomas Moore

Oh! lost! forever lost! — no more
  Shall Vesper light our dewy way
Along the rocks of Crissa's shore,
  To hymn the fading fires of day!
No more to Tempe's distant vale
  In holy musings shall we roam,
Through summer's glow and winter's gale,
  To bear the mystic chaplets home!
'Twas then my soul's expanding zeal,
  By Nature warmed and led by thee,
In every breeze was taught to feel
  The breathings of a deity!
Guide of my heart! to memory true,
  Thy looks, thy words, are still my own —
I see thee raising from the dew
  Some laurel, by the wind o'erthrown,
And hear thee say, " This humble bough
  Was planted for a doom divine,
And, though it weep in languor now,
  Shall flourish on the Delphic shrine!
Thus in the vale of earthly sense,
  Though sunk awhile the spirit lies,
A viewless hand shall cull it thence,
  To bloom immortal in the skies! "

Thy words had such a melting flow,
  And spoke of truth so sweetly well,

They dropped like heaven's serenest snow,
   And all was brightness where they fell!
Fond soother of my infant tear!
   Fond sharer of my infant joy!
Is not thy shade still lingering here?
   Am I not still thy soul's employ?
And oh! as oft at close of day,
   When meeting on the sacred mount,
Our nymphs awaked the choral lay,
   And danced around Cassotis' fount:
As then, 'twas all thy wish and care,
   That mine should be the simplest mien,
My lyre and voice the sweetest there,
   My foot the lightest o'er the green:
So still, each little grace to mold,
   Around my form thine eyes are shed,
Arranging every snowy fold,
   And guiding every mazy tread!
And when I lead the hymning choir,
   Thy spirit still, unseen and free,
Hovers between my lips and lyre,
   And weds them into harmony!
Flow, Plistus, flow, thy murmuring wave
   Shall never drop its silvery tear
Upon so pure, so blest a grave,
   To memory so divinely dear!

ROCK ME TO SLEEP *

By Elizabeth Akers

Backward, turn backward, O Time, in your flight,
Make me a child again just for to-night!

Mother come back from the echoless shore,
Take me again to your heart as of yore;
Kiss from my forehead the furrows of care,
Smooth the few silver threads out of my hair;
Over my slumbers your loving watch keep; —
Rock me to sleep, mother,— rock me to sleep!

Backward, flow backward, O tide of the years!
I am so weary of toil and of tears,—
Toil without recompense, tears all in vain,—
Take them, and give me my childhood again!
I have grown weary of dust and decay,—
Weary of flinging my soul-wealth away;
Weary of sowing for others to reap; —
Rock me to sleep, mother,— rock me to sleep!

Tired of the hollow, the base, the untrue,
Mother, O mother, my heart calls for you!
Many a summer the grass has grown green,
Blossomed and faded, our faces between:
Yet, with strong yearning and passionate pain
Long I to-night for your presence again.
Come from the silence so long and so deep; —
Rock me to sleep, mother,— rock me to sleep!

Over my heart, in the days that are flown,
No love like mother-love ever has shone;
No other worship abides and endures,—
Faithful, unselfish, and patient like yours:
None like a mother can charm away pain
From the sick soul and world-weary brain.

Slumber's soft calms o'er my heavy lids creep; —
Rock me to sleep, mother,— rock me to sleep!

Come, let your brown hair, just lighted with gold,
Fall on your shoulders again as of old;
Let it drop over my forehead to-night,
Shading my faint eyes away from the light;
For with its sunny-edged shadows once more
Haply will throng the sweet visions of yore;
Lovingly, softly, its bright billows sweep; —
Rock me to sleep, mother,— rock me to sleep!

Mother, dear mother, the years have been long
Since I last listened your lullaby song:
Sing, then, and unto my soul it shall seem
Womanhood's years have been only a dream.
Clasped to your heart in a loving embrace,
With your light lashes just sweeping my face,
Never hereafter to wake or to weep; —
Rock me to sleep, mother,— rock me to sleep!

*From "The World's Best Poetry." A. C. McClurg & Co.

I MISS THEE, MY MOTHER

By Eliza Cook

I miss thee, my Mother! Thy image is still
    The deepest impressed on my heart,
And the tablet so faithful in death must be chill
    Ere a line of that image depart.
Thou wert torn from my side when I treasured thee
        most —

When my reason could measure thy worth;
When I knew but too well that the idol I'd lost
  Could be never replaced upon earth.

I miss thee, my Mother, in circles of joy,
  Where I've mingled with rapturous zest;
For how slight is the touch that will serve to destroy
  All the fairy web spun in my breast!
Some melody sweet may be floating around —
  'Tis a ballad I learned at thy knee;
Some strain may be played, and I shrink from the
    sound,
  For my fingers oft woke it for thee.

I miss thee, my Mother; when young health has fled,
  And I sink in the languor of pain,
Where, where is the arm that once pillowed my head,
  And the ear that once heard me complain?
Other hands may support, gentle accents may fall —
  For the fond and the true are yet mine:
I've a blessing for each; I am grateful to all —
  But whose care *can* be soothing as thine?

I miss thee, my Mother, in summer's fair day,
  When I rest in the ivy-wreathed bower,
When I hang thy pet linnet's cage high on the spray,
  Or gaze on thy favorite flower.
There's the bright gravel path where I played by thy
    side
  When time had scarce wrinkled thy brow,

Where I carefully led thee with worshiping pride
   When thy scanty locks gathered the snow.

I miss thee, my Mother, in winter's long night:
   I remember the tales thou wouldst tell —
The romance of wild fancy, the legend of fright —
   Oh! who could e'er tell them so well?
Thy corner is vacant; thy chair is removed:
   It was kind to take that from my eye:
Yet relics are round me — the sacred and loved —
   To call up the pure sorrow-fed sigh.

I miss thee, my Mother! Oh, when do I not?
   Though I know 'twas the wisdom of Heaven
That the deepest shade fell on my sunniest spot,
   And such tie of devotion was riven;
For when thou wert with me my soul was below,
   I was chained to the world I then trod;
My affections, my thoughts, were all earth-bound; but
      now
   They have followed thy spirit to God!

ABSENCE

By Nathaniel P. Willis

" The heart that we have lain near before our birth, is the
only one that cannot forget that it has loved us."

PHILIP SLINGSBY.

My birthday! O beloved mother!
My heart is with thee o'er the seas!
I did not think to count another

Before I wept upon thy knees —
Before this scroll of absent years
Was blotted with thy streaming tears.

My own I do not care to check —
I weep — albeit here alone —
As if I hung upon thy neck,
As if thy lips were on my own,
As if this full, sad heart of mine,
Were beating closely upon thine.

Four weary years! How looks she now?
What light is in those tender eyes?
What trace of time has touched the brow
Whose look is borrowed of the skies
That listen to her nightly prayer?
How is she changed since *he* was there?
Who sleeps upon her heart alway —
Whose name upon her lips is worn —
For whom the night seems made to pray —
For whom she wakes to pray at morn —
Whose sight is dim, whose heart-strings stir,
Who weeps these tears — to think of *her!*

I know not if my mother's eyes
Would find me changed in slighter things;
I've wandered beneath many skies,
And tasted of some bitter springs;
And many leaves, once fair and gay,
From youth's full flower have dropped away —
But, as these looser leaves depart,

The lessened flower gets near the core,
And when deserted quite, the heart
Takes closer what was dear of yore —
And yearns to those who loved it first —
The sunshine and the dew by which its bud was
    nursed.

Dear mother! dost thou love me yet?
Am I remembered in my home?
When those I love for joy are met,
Does some one wish that I would come?
Thou *dost* — I *am* beloved of thee!
But as the schoolboy numbers o'er
Night after night, the Pleiades,
And finds the stars he found before —
As turns the maiden off her token —
As counts the miser o'er his gold —
So, till life's " silver cord is broken."
Would I of thy Fond love be told.—
My heart is full — mine eyes are wet —
Dear mother! dost thou love thy long-lost wan-
    derer yet?

Oh! when the hour to meet again
Creeps on — and, speeding o'er the sea,
My heart takes up its lengthened chain,
And, link by link, draws nearer thee,
When land is hailed, and from the shore,
Comes off the blessed breath of home,
With fragrance from my mother's door
Of flowers forgotten when I come —

When port is gained, and slowly now
The old familiar paths are passed,
And entering, unconscious how,
I gaze upon thy face at last,
And run to thee, all faint and weak —
And feel thy tears upon my cheek —
Oh! if my heart break not with joy,
The light of heaven will fairer seem,
And I shall grow once more a boy,
And, mother! —'twill be like a dream
That we were parted thus for years.
And once that we have dried our tears,
How will the days seem long and bright —
To meet thee always with the morn,
And hear thy blessing every night —
Thy " dearest "— thy " first-born "—
And be no more, as now, in a strange land, forlorn.

THE DAGUERREOTYPE *

By WILLIAM VAUGHN MOODY

This, then, is she,
My mother as she looked at seventeen,
When she first met my father.   Young incredibly,
Younger than spring, without the faintest trace
Of disappointment, weariness, or tean
Upon the childlike earnestness and grace
Of the waiting face.
Those close-wound ropes of pearl
(Or common beads made precious by their use)

Seem heavy for so slight a throat to wear;
But the low bodice leaves the shoulders bare
And half the glad swell of the breast, for news
That now the woman stirs within the girl.
And yet,
Even so, the loops and globes
Of beaten gold
And jet
Hung, in the stately way of old,
From the ears' drooping lobes
On festivals and Lord's-day of the week,
Show all too matron-sober for the cheek,—
Which, now I look again, is perfect child,
Or no — or no — 'tis girlhood's very self,
Molded by some deep, mischief-ridden elf
So meek, so maiden mild,
But startling the close gazer with the sense
Of passion forest-shy and forest-wild,
And delicate delirious merriments.

As a moth beats sidewise
And up and over, and tries
To skirt the irresistible lure
Of the flame that has him sure,
My spirit, that is none too strong to-day,
Flutters and makes delay,—
Pausing to wonder at the perfect lips,
Lifting to muse upon the low-drawn hair
And each hid radiance there,
But powerless to stem the tide-race bright,
The vehement peace which drifts it toward the light

Where soon — ah, now, with cries
Of grief and giving-up unto its gain
It shrinks no longer nor denies,
But dips
Hurriedly home to the exquisite heart of pain,—
And all is well, for I have seen them plain,
The unforgettable, the unforgotten eyes!
Across the blinding gush of these good tears
They shine as in the sweet and heavy years
When by her bed and chair
We children gathered jealously to share
The sunlit aura breathing myrrh and thyme,
Where the sore-stricken body made a clime
Gentler than May and pleasanter than rhyme,
Holier and more mystical than prayer.

God, how thy ways are strange!
That this should be, even this,
The patient head
Which suffered years ago the dreary change!
That these so dewy lips should be the same
As those I stooped to kiss
And heard my harrowing half-spoken name,
A little ere the one who bowed above her,
Our father and her very constant lover,
Rose stoical, and we knew that she was dead.
Then I, who could not understand or share
His antique nobleness,
Being unapt to bear
The insults which time flings us for our proof,
Fled from the horrible roof

Into the alien sunshine merciless,
The shrill satiric fields ghastly with day,
Raging to front God in his pride of sway
And hurl across the lifted swords of fate
That ringed Him where He sat
My puny gage of scorn and desolate hate
Which somehow should undo Him, after all!
That this girl face, expectant, virginal,
Which gazes out at me
Boon as a sweetheart, as if nothing loth
(Save for the eyes, with other presage stored)
To pledge me troth,
And in the kingdom where the heart is lord
Take sail on the terrible gladness of the deep
Whose winds the gray Norns keep,—
That this should be indeed
The flesh which caught my soul, a flying seed,
Out of the to and fro
Of scattering hands where the seedsman Mage,
Stooping from star to star and age to age
Sings as he sows!
That underneath this breast
Nine moons I fed
Deep of divine unrest,
While over and over in the dark she said,
" Blessèd! but not as happier children blessed "—
That this should be
Even she . . .
God, how with time and change
Thou makest thy footsteps strange!
Ah, now I know

They play upon me, and it is not so.
Why, 'tis a girl I never saw before,
A little thing to flatter and make weep,
To tease until her heart is sore,
Then kiss and clear the score;
A gypsy run-the-fields,
A little liberal daughter of the earth,
Good for what hour of truancy and mirth
The careless season yields
Hither-side the flood of the year and yonder of the
    neap;
Then thank you, thanks again, and twenty light good-
    byes.—
O shrined above the skies,
Frown not, clear brow,
Darken not, holy eyes!
Thou knowest well I know that it is thou
Only to save from such memories
As would unman me quite,
Here in this web of strangeness caught
And prey to troubled thought
Do I devise
These foolish shifts and slight;
Only to shield me from the afflicting sense
Of some waste influence
Which from this morning face and lustrous hair
Breathes on me sudden ruin and despair.
In any other guise,
With any but this girlish depth of gaze,
Your coming had not so unsealed and poured
The dusty amphoras where I had stored

The drippings of the winepress of my days.
I think these eyes foresee,
Now in their unawakened virgin time,
Their mother's pride in me,
And dream even now, unconsciously,
Upon each soaring peak and sky-hung lea
You pictured I should climb.
Broken premonitions come,
Shapes, gestures visionary,
Not as once to maiden Mary
The manifest angel with fresh lilies came
Intelligibly calling her by name;
But vanishingly, dumb,
Thwarted and bright and wild,
As heralding a sin-defiled,
Earth-encumbered, blood-begotten, passionate man-
    child,
Who yet should be a trump of mighty call
Blown in the gates of evil kings
To make them fall;
Who yet should be a sword of flame before
The soul's inviolate door
To beat away the clang of hellish wings;
Who yet should be a lyre
Of high unquenchable desire
In the day of little things.—
Look where the amphoras,
The yield of many days,
Trod by my hot soul from the pulp of self,
And set upon the shelf
In sullen pride

The Vineyard-master's tasting to abide —
O mother mine!
Are these the bringings-in, the doings fine,
Of him you used to praise?
Emptied and overthrown
The jars lie strown.
These, for their flavor duly nursed,
Drip from the stopples vinegar accursed;
These, I thought honied to the very seal,
Dry, dry,— a little acid meal,
A pinch of moldy dust,
Sole leavings of the amber-mantling must;
These rude to look upon,
But flasking up the liquor dearest won,
Through sacred hours and hard,
With watchings and with wrestlings and with grief,
Even of these, of these in chief,
The stale breath sickens reeking from the shard.
Nothing is left. Aye, how much less than naught!
What shall be said or thought
Of the slack hours and waste imaginings,
The cynic rending of the wings,
Known to the froward, that unreckoning heart
Whereof this brewage was the precious part,
Treasured and set away with furtive boast?
O dear and cruel ghost,
Be merciful, be just!
See, I was yours and I am in the dust.
Then look not so, as if all things were well!
Take your eyes from me, leave me to my shame,
Or else, if gaze they must,

Steel them with judgment, darken them with blame;
But by the ways of light ineffable
You bade me go and I have faltered from,
By the low waters moaning out of hell
Whereto my feet have come,
Lay not on me these intolerable
Looks of rejoicing love, of pride, of happy trust!

Nothing dismayed?
By all I say and all I hint not made
Afraid?
O then, stay by me!   Let
These eyes afflict me, cleanse me, keep me yet,
Brave eyes and true!
See how the shriveled heart, that long has lain
Dead to delight and pain,
Stirs, and begins again
To utter pleasant life, as if it knew
The wintry days were through;
As if in its awakening boughs it heard
The quick, sweet-spoken bird.
Strong eyes and brave,
Inexorable to save!

*"The Little Book of Modern American Verse." Houghton Mifflin Company.

IV

MOTHER TO CHILD

ON A SEVENTEENTH BIRTHDAY *

By Anne P. L. Field

To-day my tall broad-shouldered lad,
  With such a grave, protective mien,
I watched with eyes grown strangely sad,
  Though proud these mother-eyes had been,—
  For brave and bonny seventeen
Is not a saddening sight to see,
  Yet I have lost, long years between,
My little boy that used to be!

How well-remembered and how glad
  That hour when happier than a queen
A rosy infant son I had,
  When all the singing world was green;
  With what deep gratitude serene
I welcomed my maternity —
  He was the sweetest ever seen —
My little boy that used to be!

I see him now in velvet clad —
  And just a trifle vain, I ween,—
Showing his new suit to his " dad,"
  As male birds their fine feathers preen.
  His curls had such a golden sheen,

And by his crib on bended knee
   I'd pray God's love from harm would screen
My little boy that used to be!

Envoy

O son upon whose strength I lean,
   Be very patient, dear, with me,
For mothers miss with anguish keen
   The little boy that used to be!

* Reprinted by courtesy of " The Youth's Companion."

MY SONG *

By Rabindranath Tagore

This song of mine will wind its music around you, my child, like the fond arms of love.

This song of mine will touch your forehead like a kiss of blessing.

When you are alone it will sit by your side and whisper in your ear, when you are in the crowd it will fence you about with aloofness.

My song will be like a pair of wings to your dreams, it will transport your heart to the verge of the unknown.

It will be like a faithful star overhead when dark night is over your road.

My song will sit in the pupils of your eyes, and will carry your sight into the heart of things.

And when my voice is silent in death, my song will speak in your living heart.

* Copyrighted 1913 by The Macmillan Company.

THE GIFT *

By Rabindranath Tagore

I want to give you something my child, for we are drifting in the stream of the world.   Our lives will be carried apart, and our love forgotten.   But I am not so foolish as to hope that I could buy your heart with gifts.   Young is your life, your path long, and you drink the love we bring you at one draught and turn and run away from us.   You have your play and your playmates.   What harm is there if you have no time or thought for us?

We, indeed, have leisure enough in old age to count the days that are past, to cherish in our hearts what our hands have lost forever.

The river runs swift with a song, breaking through all barriers.   But the mountain stays and remembers, and follows her with his love.

* Copyrighted 1913 by The Macmillan Company.

BABY'S WAY *

By Rabindranath Tagore

If baby only wanted to, he could fly up to heaven this moment.

It is not for nothing that he does not leave us.

He loves to rest his head on mother's bosom, and cannot ever bear to lose sight of her.

Baby knows all manner of wise words, though few on earth can understand their meaning.

It is not for nothing that he never wants to speak.

The one thing he wants is to learn mother's words from mother's lips.   That is why he looks so innocent.

Baby had a heap of gold and pearls, yet he came like a beggar on to this earth.   It is not for nothing that he came in such a disguise.

This dear little naked mendicant pretends to be utterly helpless, so that he may beg for mother's wealth of love.

Baby was so free from every tie in the land of the tiny crescent moon.   It was not for nothing he gave up his freedom.

He knows that there is room for endless joy in mother's little corner of a heart, and it is sweeter far than liberty to be caught and pressed in her dear arms.

Baby never knew how to cry.   He dwelt in the land of perfect bliss.

It is not for nothing he has chosen to shed tears.

Though with the smile of his dear face he draws mother's yearning heart to him, yet his little cries over tiny troubles weave the double bond of pity and love.

Copyrighted 1913 by The Macmillan Company.

THE RECALL *

By Rabindranath Tagore

The night was dark when she went away, and they slept.

The night is dark now, and I call for her, " Come back, my darling; the world is asleep; and no one would know, if you came for a moment while stars are gazing at stars."

She went away when the trees were in bud and the spring was young.

Now the flowers are in high bloom and I call, " Come back, my darling. The children gather and scatter flowers in reckless sport. And if you come and take one little blossom no one will miss it."

Those that used to play are playing still, so spend-thrift is life.

I listen to their chatter and call, " Come back, my darling, for mother's heart is full to the brim with love, and if you come to snatch only one little kiss from her no one will grudge it."

SOME TIME *

By Eugene Field

Last night, my darling, as you slept,
  I thought I heard you sigh,
And to your little crib I crept,
  And watched a space thereby;
Then, bending down, I kissed your brow —
  For, oh! I love you so —
You are too young to know it now,
  But some time you shall know.

Some time, when, in a darkened place
  Where others come to weep,
Your eyes shall see a weary face
  Calm in eternal sleep;
The speechless lips, the wrinkled brow,
  The patient smile may show —

You are too young to know it now,
But some time you shall know.

Look backward, then, into the years,
And see me here to-night —
See, O my darling! how my tears
Are falling as I write;
And feel once more upon your brow
The kiss of long ago —
You are too young to know it now,
But some time you shall know.

By courtesy of Charles Scribner's Sons.

MY BIRD

By Emily C. Judson

(Lines written at Burmah in joy for a first-born)

Ere last year's morn had left the sky,
A birdling sought my Indian nest;
And folded, oh, so lovingly,
Her tiny wings upon my breast.

From morn till evening's purple tinge,
In winsome helplessness she lies;
Two rose leaves with a silken fringe,
Shut softly on her starry eyes.

There's not in Ind a lovelier bird;
Broad earth owns not a happier nest;
O God, thou hast a fountain stirred,
Whose waters never more shall rest.

This beautiful, mysterious thing,
  This seeming visitant from heaven,
This bird with the immortal wing,
  To me, to me, thy hand has given.

The pulse first caught its tiny stroke,
  The blood its crimson hue, from mine; —
This life which I have dared invoke,
  Henceforth, is parallel with thine.

A silent awe is in my room,
  I tremble with delicious fear;
The future, with its light and gloom,
  Time and eternity are here.

Doubts, hopes, in eager tumult rise,
  Hear, O my God, one earnest prayer:
Room for my bird in Paradise,
  And give her angel-plumage there.

FROM " NIOBE " *

By Frederick Tennyson

I too, remember, in the after years,
The long-hair'd Niobe, when she was old,
Sitting alone, without the city gates,
Upon the ground; alone she sat, and mourn'd.
Her watches, mindful of her royal state,
Her widowhood, and sorrows, follow'd her
Far off, when she went forth, to be alone

In lonely places; and at set of sun
They won her back by some fond phantasy,
By telling her some tale of the gone days
Of her dear lost ones, promising to show her
Some faded garland, or some broken toy,
Dusty and dim, which they had found, or feign'd
To have found, some plaything of their infant hours.
Within the echoes of a ruin'd court
She sat and mourn'd, with her lamenting voice,
Melodious in sorrow, like the sound
Of funeral hymns; for in her youth she sang
Along the myrtle valleys in the spring,
Plucking the fresh pinks and the hyacinths,
With her fair troop of girls, who answer'd her
Silvery sweet, so that the lovely tribe
Were Nature's matchless treble to the last
Delicious pipe, pure, warbling, dewy clear.
In summer and in winter, that lorn voice
Went up, like the struck spirit of this world,
Making the starry roof of heaven tremble
With her lament, and agony, and all
The crowned Gods in their high tabernacles
Sigh unawares, and think upon their deeds.
Her guardians let her wander at her will,
For all could weep for her; had she not been
The first and fairest of that sunny land,
And bless'd with all things; doubly crown'd with power
And beauty, doubly now discrown'd and fallen?
Oh! none would harm her, only she herself;
And chiefly then when they would hold her back,
And sue her to take comfort in her home,

Or in the bridal chambers of her youth,
Or in the old gardens, once her joy and pride,
Or the rose-bowers along the river-shore
She lov'd of old, now silent and forsaken.
For then she fled away, as though in fear,
As if she saw the specters of her hours
Of joyance pass before her in the shapes
Of her belov'd ones.   But most she chose
Waste places, where the moss and lichen crawl'd,
And the wild ivy flutt'd, and the rains
Wept thro' the roofless ruins, and all seem'd
To mourn in symbols, and to answer to her,
Showing her outward that she was within.
The unregarding multitude pass'd on,
Because her woe was a familiar sight.
But some there were that shut their ears and fled,
And they were childless; the rose-lipp'd and young
Felt that imperial voice and desolate
Strike cold into their hearts; children at play
Were smit with sudden silence, with their toys
Clutch'd in their hands, forgetful of the game.
Aged she was, yet beautiful in age.
Her beauty, thro' the cloud of years and grief,
Shone as a wintry sun; she never smil'd,
Save when a darkness pass'd across the sun,
And blotted out from her entranced eyes
Disastrous shapes that rode upon his disk,
Tyrannous visions, armed presences;
And then she sigh'd and lifted up her head,
And shed a few warm tears.   But when he rose,
And her sad eyes unclos'd before his beams,

She started up with terrors in her look,
That wither'd up all pity in affright,
And ran about, like one with Furies torn,
And rent her hair, and madly threaten'd Heaven,
And called for retribution on the gods,
Crying, "O save me from Him, He is there;
Oh, let me wear my little span of life.
I see Him in the center of the sun;
His face is black with wrath! thou angry God,
I am a worthless thing, a childless mother,
Widow'd and wasted, old and comfortless,
But still I am alive; wouldst thou take all?
Thou who hast snatch'd my hopes and my delights,
Thou who hast kill'd my children, wouldst thou take
The little remnant of my days of sorrow,
Which the sharp winds of the first winter days,
Or the first night of frost, may give unto thee?
For never shall I seek again that home
Where they are not; cold, cold shall be the hearth
Where they were gather'd, cold as is my heart!
Oh, if my living lot be bitterness,
'Tis sweeter than to think, that, if I go
Down to the dust, then I shall think no more
Of them I lov'd and lost, the thoughts of whom
Are all my being, and shall speak no more,
In answer to their voices in my heart,
As though it were mine ear, rewording all
Their innocent delights, and fleeting pains,
Their infant fondnesses, their little wants,
And simple words.   Oh! while I am, I dream
Of those who are not; thus my anguish grows

My solace, as the salt surf of the seas
Clothes the sharp crags with beauty." Then her mood
Would veer to madness, like a windy change
That brings up thunder, and she rais'd her voice,
Crying, " And yet they are not, they who were,
And never more shall be! accursed dreams!"
And, suddenly becoming motionless,
The bright hue from her cheeks and forehead pass'd,
And full of awful resignation, fixing
Her large undazzled orbs upon the sun,
She shrieked, " Strike, God, thou canst not harm me
  more!"

From " The Victorian Anthology." Houghton, Mifflin Company.

FROM THE PLEA OF CORNELIA

By Propertius

English version by E. D. A. Morshead

Guard, Paullus, guard the pledges of our love —
My very dust that ingrained wish can move!
Father thou art, and mother must thou be,
Unto those little ones bereft of me.
Weep they, give two-fold kisses, thine and mine,
Solace their hearts, and both our loves combine;
And if thou needst must weep, go, weep apart —
Let not our children, folded to thine heart,
Between thy kisses feel the teardrops start.
Enough for love, be nightlong thoughts of me,
And phantom forms that murmur I am she.
Or if thou speakest to mine effigy,
Speak soft, and pause and dream of a reply.

Yet — if a presence new our halls behold,
And a new bride my wonted place shall hold —
My children, speak her fair, who pleased your sire,
And let your gentleness disarm her ire:
Nor speak in praise of me — your loyal part
Will turn to gall and wormwood in her heart.
But, if your father hold my worth so high,
That lifelong love can people vacancy,
And solitude seem only love gone by,
Tend ye his loneliness, his thoughts engage,
And bar the avenues of pain to age!
I died before my time — add my lost years
Unto your youth, be to his heart compeers;
So shall he face, content, life's slow decline,
Glad in my children's love, as once in mine.

THE ABSENT SOLDIER SON

By Sidney Dobell

Lord, I am weeping. As Thou wilt, O Lord,
Do with him as Thou wilt; but O my God,
Let him come back to die! Let not the fowls
O' the air defile the body of my child,
My own fair child, that when he was a babe,
I lift up in my arms and gave to Thee!
Let not his garment, Lord, be vilely parted,
Nor the fine linen which these hands have spun
Fall to the stranger's lot! Shall the wild bird,
That would have pilfered of the ox, this year
Disdain the pens and stalls? Shall her blind young

That on the fleck and moult of brutish beasts
Had been too happy, sleep in cloth of gold
Whereof each thread is to this beating heart
As a peculiar darling?   Lo, the flies
Hum o'er him! lo, a feather from the crow
Falls in his parted lips!   Lo, his dead eyes
See not the raven!   Lo, the worm, the worm,
Creeps from his festering corse?   My God! my God!

.   .   .   .

O Lord, Thou doest well.   I am content.
If Thou have need of him he shall not stay.
But as one calleth to a servant, saying
" At such a time be with me," so, O Lord,
Call him to Thee!   O, bid him not in haste
Straight whence he standeth.   Let him lay aside
The soiléd tools of labor.   Let him wash
His hands of blood.   Let him array himself
Meet for his Lord, pure from the sweat and fume
Of corporal travail!   Lord, if he must die,
Let him die here.   O, take him where Thou gavest!

THE MOTHER'S HOPE

By Laman Blanchard

Is there, when the winds are singing
    In the happy summer-time,—
When the raptured air is ringing
With Earth's music heavenward springing,
    Forest chirp, and village chime,—
Is there, of the sounds that float

Unsighingly, a single note
Half so sweet and clear and wild
As the laughter of a child?

Listen! and be now delighted:
    Morn hath touched her golden strings;
Earth and Sky their vows have plighted;
Life and light are reunited
    Amid countless carollings;
    Yet, delicious as they are,
There's a sound that's sweeter far,—
One that makes the heart rejoice
More than all,—the human voice!

Organ finer, deeper, clearer,
    Though it be a stranger's tone,—
Than the winds or waters dearer,
More enchanting to the hearer,
    For it answereth to his own.
But, of all its witching words,
Sweeter than the song of birds,
Those are sweetest, bubbling wild
Through the laughter of a child.

Harmonies from time-touched towers,
    Haunted strains from rivulets,
Hum of bees among the flowers,
Rustling leaves, and silver showers,—
    These, ere long, the ear forgets;
But in mine there is a sound
Ringing on the whole year round,—

Heart-deep laughter that I heard
Ere my child could speak a word.

Ah! 'twas heard by ear far purer,
    Fondlier formed to catch the strain,—
Ear of one whose love is surer,—
Hers, the mother, the endurer
    Of the deepest share of pain;
Hers the deepest bliss to treasure
Memories of that cry of pleasure,
Hers to hoard, a lifetime after,
Echoes of that infant laughter.

'Tis a mother's large affection
    Hears with a mysterious sense,—
Breathings that evade detection,
Whisper faint, and fine inflection,
    Thrill in her with power intense.
Childhood's honeyed words untaught
Hiveth she in loving thought,—
Tones that never thence depart;
For she listens — with her heart.

THE MOTHER'S HEART

By Mrs. Norton

When first thou camest, gentle, shy, and fond,
    My eldest-born, first hope, and dearest treasure,
My heart received thee with a joy beyond
    All that it yet had felt of earthly pleasure;

Nor thought that any love again might be
So deep and strong as that I felt for thee.

Faithful and true, with sense beyond thy years,
    And natural piety that leaned to heaven;
Wrung by a harsh word suddenly to tears,
    Yet patient to rebuke when justly given;
Obedient, easy to be reconciled,
And meekly cheerful; such wert thou, my child!

Not willing to be left — still by my side,
    Haunting my walks, while summer-day was dying
Nor leaving in thy turn, but pleased to glide
    Through the dark room where I was sadly lying;
Or by the couch of pain, a sitter meek,
Watch the dim eye, and kiss the fevered cheek.

O boy! of such as thou are oftenest made
    Earth's fragile idols; like a tender flower,
No strength in all freshness, prone to fade,
    And bending weakly to the thunder-shower;
Still, round the loved, thy heart found force to bind,
And clung, like woodbine shaken in the wind!

Then THOU, my merry love,— bold in thy glee,
    Under the bough, or by the firelight dancing,
With thy sweet temper, and thy spirit free,—
    Didst come, as restless as a bird's wing glancing,
Full of a wild and irrepressible mirth,
Like a young sunbeam to the gladdened earth!

Thine was the shout, the song, the burst of joy,
  Which sweet from childhood's rosy lip resoundeth;
Thine was the eager spirit naught could cloy,
  And the glad heart from which all grief reboundeth;
And many a mirthful jest and mock reply
Lurked in the laughter of thy dark-blue eye.

And thine was many an art to win and bless,
  The cold and stern to joy and fondness warming;
The coaxing smile, the frequent soft caress,
  The earnest, tearful prayer all wrath disarming!
Again my heart a new affection found,
But thought that love with thee had reached its bound.

At length THOU camest,— thou, the last and least,
  Nicknamed " the Emperor " by thy laughing brothers,
Because a haughty spirit swelled thy breast,
  And thou didst seek to rule and sway the others,
Mingling with every playful infant wile
A mimic majesty that made us smile.

And O, most like a regal child wert thou!
  An eye of resolute and successful scheming!
Fair shoulders, curling lips, and dauntless brow,
  Fit for the world's strife, not for poet's dreaming;
And proud the lifting of thy stately head,
And the firm bearing of thy conscious tread.

Different from both! yet each succeeding claim
  I, that all other love had been forswearing,
Forthwith admitted, equal and the same;
  Nor injured either by this love's comparing,

Nor stole a fraction for the newer call,—
But in the mother's heart found room for all!

THE SAD MOTHER

By Katharine Tynan Hinkson

O when the half-light weaves
    Wild shadows on the floor,
How ghostly come the withered leaves
    Stealing about my door!

I sit and hold my breath,
    Lone in the lonely house;
Naught breaks the silence still as death,
    Only a creeping mouse.

The patter of leaves, it may be,
    But liker patter of feet,
The small feet of my own baby
    That never felt the heat.

The small feet of my son,
    Cold as the grave yard sod;
My little, dumb, unchristened one
    That may not win to God.

" Come in, dear babe," I cry,
    Opening the door so wide.
The leaves go stealing softly by;
    How dark it is outside!

And though I kneel and pray
   Long on the threshold-stone
The little feet press on their way,
   And I am ever alone.

NUSAIB *

TRANSLATION OF C. J. LYALL FROM THE ARABIC

They said last night — to-morrow at first of dawning,
   or may be at eventide, must Laila go! —
My heart at the word lay helpless, as lies a *Kata* in net
   night-long, and struggles with fast-bound wing.
Two nestlings she left alone, in a nest far distant, a
   nest which the winds smite, tossing it to and fro.
They hear but the whistling breeze, and stretch necks to
   greet her but she they await — the end of her days
   is come!
So lies she, and neither gains in the night her longing,
   nor brings her the morning any release from pain.

* By permission of the publishers of The Warner Library of the World's Best Literature.

LAMENT

BY RODEN NOEL

I am lying in thy tomb, love,
   Lying in thy tomb,
Tho' I move within the gloom, love,
   Breathe within the gloom!
Men deem life not fled, dear,
   Deem my life not fled,
Tho' I with thee am dead, dear,

I with thee am dead,
O my little child.

What is the gray world, darling,
What is the gray world,
Where the worm lies curl'd, darling,
The deathworm lies curl'd?
They tell me of the spring, dear!
Do I want the spring?
Will she waft upon her wing, dear,
The joy-pulse of her wing,
Thy songs, thy blossoming,
O my little child.

For the hallowing of thy smile, love,
The rainbow of thy smile,
Gleaming for awhile, love,
Gleaming to beguile,
Replunged me in the cold, dear,
Leaves me in the cold.
And I feel so very old, dear,
Very, very old!

Would they put me out of pain, dear,
Out of all my pain,
Since I may not live again, dear,
Never live again!

I am lying in the grave, love,
In thy little grave,
Yet I hear the wind rave, love,

And the wild wave!
I would lie asleep, darling,
With thee lie asleep,
Unhearing the world weep, darling,
Little children weep!
O my little child!

THE PATRIOT MOTHER

IRISH BALLAD 1798

" Come tell us the name of the rebelly crew
Who lifted the pike on the Curragh with you;
Come, tell us their treason, and then you'll be free,
Or by heavens you shall swing from the high gallows
    tree."

" *Alanna! alanna!* * the shadow of shame
Has never yet fallen on one of your name,
And, oh! may the food from my bosom you drew,
In your veins turn to poison, if *you* prove untrue.

" The foul words — oh! let them not blacken your
    tongue,
That would prove to your friends and your country a
    wrong,
Or the curse of a mother, so bitter and dread,
With the wrath of the Lord — may they fall on your
    head!

* Alanna — beauty " My beautiful! "

" I have no one but you in the whole world wide,
Yet, false to your pledge, you'd ne'er stand by my side;
If a traitor you liv'd, you'd be farther away
From my heart than, if true, you were wrapped in the
    clay.

" Oh! deeper and darker the mourning would be
For your falsehood so base, than your death proud and
    free;
Dearer, far dearer than ever to me,
My darling, you'll be on the brave gallows tree.

" 'Tis holy, *agra!* † with the bravest and best
Go! go! from my heart, and be joined with the rest;
Alanna ma cree! O, alanna ma cree! ‡
Sure a ' *stag* ' ¶ and a traitor you never will be."

There's no look of a traitor upon the young brow
That's raised to the tempters so haughtily now;
No traitor e'er held up the firm head so high —
No traitor e'er show'd such a proud flashing eye.

On the high gallows tree! on the brave gallows tree!
Where smil'd leaves and blossoms, his sad doom met
    he;
But it never bore blossom so pure and so fair,
As the heart of the martyr that hangs from it there.

† My love.
‡ Beauty of my heart.
¶ An informer.

A MOTHER IN EGYPT

By Marjorie L. C. Pickthall

*" About midnight will I go out into the midst of Egypt:
and all the first-born in the land of Egypt shall die, from the
first-born of Pharaoh that sitteth upon his throne, even unto
the first-born of the maid-servant that is behind the mill."*

Is the noise of grief in the palace over the river
For this silent one at my side?
There came a hush in the night, and he rose with his
　　hands a-quiver
Like lotus petals adrift on the swing of the tide.
O small cold hands, the day groweth old for sleeping!
O small still feet, rise up, for the hour is late!
Rise up, my son, for I hear them mourning and weep-
　　ing
In the temple down by the the gate!

Hushed is the face that was wont to brighten with
　　laughter
When I sang at the mill;
And silence unbroken shall greet the sorrowful dawns
　　hereafter,—
The house shall be still.
Voice after voice takes up the burden of wailing —
Do you not heed, do you not hear? — in the high
　　priest's house by the wall.
But mine is the grief, and their sorrow is all unavail-
　　ing.
Will he awake at their call?

Something I saw of the broad dim wings half folding
The passionless brow.
Something I saw of the sword that the shadowy hands
     were holding,—
What matters it now?
I held you close, dear face, as I knelt and harkened
To the wind that cried last night like a soul in sin,
When the broad bright stars dropped down and the
     soft sky darkened
And the presence moved therein.

I have heard men speak in the market-place of the
     city,
Low-voiced, in a breath,
Of a God who is stronger than ours, and who knows
     not changing nor pity,
Whose anger is death.
Nothing I know of the lords of the outland races,
But Amud is gentle and Hathor the mother is mild,
And who would descend from the light of the Peace-
     ful Places
To war on a child?
Yet here he lies, with a scarlet pomegranate petal
Blown down on his cheek.
The slow sun sinks to the sand like a shield of some
     burnished metal,
But he does not speak.
I have called, I have sung, but he neither will hear
     nor waken;
So lightly, so whitely, he lies in the curve of my arm,

Like a feather let fall from the bird the arrow hath
    taken,—
Who could see him, and harm?

" The swallow flies home to her sleep in the eaves of
    the altar,
And the crane to her nest."—
So do we sing o'er the mill, and why, ah, why should
    I falter,
Since he goes to his rest?
Does he play in their flowers as he played among these
    with his mother?
Do the gods smile downward and love him and give
    him their care?
Guard him well, O ye gods, till I come; lest the wrath
    of that Other
Should reach to him there.

THE FAREWELL

Of a Virginia Slave Mother to Her Daughters Sold
Into Southern Bondage.

By John Greenleaf Whittier

Gone, gone,— sold and gone,
    To the rice-swamps dank and lone.
Where the slave whip ceaseless swings,
Where the noisome insect stings,
Where the fever demon strews

Poison with the falling dews,
Where the sickly sunbeams glare
Through the hot and misty air,—
    Gone, gone,— sold and gone,
    To the rice-swamps dank and lone,
    From Virginia's hills and waters,—
    Woe is me, my stolen daughters!

    Gone, gone,— sold and gone,
    To the rice-swamps dank and lone.
There no mother's eye is near them,
There no mother's ear can hear them;
Never, when the torturing lash
Seams their back with many a gash,
Shall a mother's kindness bless them;
Or a mother's arms caress them.
    Gone, gone,— sold and gone,
    To the rice-swamps dank and lone,
    From Virginia's hills and waters,—
    Woe is me, my stolen daughters!

    Gone, gone,— sold and gone,
    To the rice-swamps dank and lone.
From the tree whose shadow lay
On their childhood's place of play,—
From the cool spring where they drank,—
Rock, and hill, and rivulet bank,—
From the solemn house of prayer,
And the holy counsels there,—

Gone, gone,— sold and gone,
To the rice-swamps dank and lone,
From Virginia's hills and waters,—
Woe is me, my stolen daughters!

Gone, gone,— sold and gone,
To the rice-swamps dank and lone.
Toiling through the weary day,
And at night the spoilers prey.
O that they had earlier died,
Sleeping calmly, side by side,
Where the tyrant's power is o'er,
And the fetter galls no more!
Gone, gone,— sold and gone,
To the rice-swamps dank and lone,
From Virginia's hills and waters,—
Woe is me, my stolen daughters!

Gone, gone,— sold and gone,
To the rice-swamps dank and lone.
By the holy love he beareth,—
By the bruised reed he spareth,—
O, may He, to whom alone
All the cruel wrongs are known,
Still their hope and refuge prove,
With a more than mother's love.
Gone, gone,— sold and gone,
To the rice-swamps dank and lone,
From Virginia's hills and waters,—
Woe is me, my stolen daughters!

AN ABORIGINAL MOTHER'S LAMENT
By Charles Harpur

Still farther would I fly, my child,
  To make thee safer yet,
From the unsparing white man,
  With his dread hand murder-wet!
I'll bear thee on as I have borne
  With stealthy steps wind-fleet,
But the dark night shrouds the forest,
  And thorns are in my feet.

O moan not! I would give this braid —
  Thy father's gift to me —
But for a single palmful
  Of water now for thee.

Ah! spring not to his name — no more
  To glad us may he come —
He is smoldering into ashes
  Beneath the blasted gum:
All charred and blasted by the fire
  The white man kindled there,
And fed with our slaughtered kindred
  Till heaven-high went its glare!

And but for thee, I would their fire
  Had eaten me as fast!
Hark! Hark! I hear his death-cry
  Yet lengthening up the blast!

But no — when his bound hands had signed
  The way that we should fly,
On the roaring pyre flung bleeding —
  I saw thy father die!

No more shall his loud tomahawk
  Be plied to win our cheer,
Or the shining fish pools darken
  Beneath his shadowing spear:
The fading tracks of his fleet foot
  Shall guide not as before,
And the mountain-spirits mimic
  His hunting call no more!

O moan not! I would give this braid —
  Thy father's gift to me —
For but a single palmful
  Of water now for thee.

HOW'S MY BOY?

By Sidney Dobell

"Ho, Sailor of the sea!
How's my boy — my boy?"
"What's your boy's name, good wife,
And in what good ship sail'd he?"
"My boy John —
He that went to sea —
What care I for the ship, sailor?
My boy's my boy to me.

You come back from sea,
And not know my John?
I might as well have ask'd some landsman
Yonder down in the town.
There's not an ass in all the parish
But he knows my John.

" How's my boy — my boy?
And unless you let me know
I'll swear you are no sailor,
Blue jacket or no,
Brass buttons or no, sailor,
Anchor or crown or no!
Sure his ship was the ' *Jolly Briton* ' "—
" Speak low, woman, speak low! "
" And why should I speak low, sailor,
About my own boy John?
If I was loud as I am proud
I'd sing him over the town!
Why should I speak low, sailor? "
" That good ship went down. "

" How's my boy — my boy?
What care I for the ship, sailor?
I was never aboard her.
Be she afloat or be she aground,
Sinking or swimming, I'll be bound,
Her owners can afford her!
I say how's my John? "
" Every man on board went down,
Every man aboard her. "

" How's my boy — my boy?
What care I for the men, sailor?
I'm not their mother —
How's my boy — my boy?
Tell me of him and no other!
How's my boy — my boy?"

V

MOTHER AND CHILD

HER FIRST-BORN

By Charles Tennyson Turner

It was her first sweet child, her heart's delight:
And, though we all foresaw his early doom,
We kept the fearful secret out of sight;
We saw the canker, but she kiss'd the bloom.
And yet it might not be: we could not brook
To vex her happy heart with vague alarms,
To blanch with fear her fond intrepid look,
Or send a thrill through those encircling arms,
She smil'd upon him, waking or at rest:
She could not dream her little child would die:
She toss'd him fondly with an upward eye:
She seem'd as buoyant as a summer spray,
That dances with a blossom on its breast,
Nor knows how soon it will be borne away.

CHILD OF A DAY

By Walter Savage Landor

Child of a day, thou knowest not
The tears that overflow thine urn,
The gushing eyes that read thy lot,
Nor, if thou knewest, couldst return.
And why the wish! the pure and blest
Watch like thy mother o'er thy sleep.
O peaceful night! O envied rest!
Thou wilt not ever see her weep.

BABY'S SKIES

By M. C. Bartlett

Would you know the baby's skies?
Baby's skies are mother's eyes.
Mother's eyes and smile together
Make the baby's pleasant weather.

Mother, keep your eyes from tears,
Keep your heart from foolish fears.
Keep your lips from dull complaining
Lest the baby think 't is raining.

ON A PICTURE OF AN INFANT PLAYING
NEAR A PRECIPICE

From the Greek of Leonidas of Alexandria, Translated by Samuel Rogers

While on a cliff with calm delight she kneels,
    And the blue vales a thousand joys recall,
See, to the last, last verge her infant steals!
    O, fly — yet stir not, speak not, lest it fall.—
Far better taught, she lays her bosom bare,
And the fond boy springs back to nestle there.

HIS MOTHER'S APRON-STRINGS *

By Isabel C. Barrows

They were never taut, unless, when he was a little
boy he used them as thongs to bind her as the " white

captive" when they played Indian. Indeed, his mother was sometimes criticised because she held them too slack, leaving the little fellow to his own devices. Her fear that when the hour of freedom struck he might slash and toss them away in the joy of independence had influenced her to give him a share of that independence as the childish years melted into youth and youth approached manhood. "You are spoiling him," folks said, but her instinct was her safe guide. The boy might be restrained by love, but not by bonds which by and by he could break.

So the years sped and the friendship between mother and son strengthened, and the ties that bound them to each other held firmer as life hurried on. He had not been given to her by birth, though his baby head had rested on her breast, but the dear mother who bore him and died could not have loved him more.

People said — poor people who did not know the joys of adoption on both sides —" How queer that he should still be tied to her apron-strings!" They did not say which was the slave, because there seemed really no compulsion either way, the strings were so slack.

It was always the same — when he was in school in France (sending her a postal card every day) or at boarding-school, in his own land; in the public high school, or at college; in the university, or away in the forest and among the mountains busy with Government duties, the bonds that held the mother and son together were lightly worn, yet through them ran an electric cord that pulsed as it felt the heart-beats of the two.

The mother was twoscore when the baby boy came into her arms. She is now nearly threescore and ten. The Psalmist's limit stands in full sight of her unabated vision. The son is in the prime of his strength. I saw them the other day as I passed through Canada. Which one had gathered up the apron-strings and drawn the other I could not tell, but here they were, one coming from the South and one from the East, for ten days of Indian summer on a Northern lake. I accepted their hospitality and saw the comradeship between them.

A log cabin with an open fire was their shelter. The surrounding hills were gleaming with frost and the mountain tops were hooded with snow, but the sun smiled on the wintry landscape, as the fire in the cabin cheered the hearth. Life in this little camp was at its simplest. A farm a mile away supplied milk, butter, eggs, and honey, and a neglected garden still held potatoes, beets, carrots, and onions, all to be roasted in the hot cinders and ashes, while a shivering cabbage yielded up its heart for salad. Biscuit browned before the fire and drenched with cream and maple syrup made the " guiltless feast " as Goldsmith's hermit calls it, surpass those described by the Latin poets. Agate-ware dishes, washed and wiped in companionship by mother and son, matched the homely fare. Ticks filled with oat straw, with heavy blankets, furnished the beds, whose only luxury consisted of white-covered pillows.

Peace reigned within and without. No human sound reached the cabin hidden in the woods. The wild things drew near unafraid, for no gun would frighten them thence. Loons and ducks plashed in the cold water of the lake. Wild geese honked their way southward in a great " V " overhead. In the cedar-bush partridges were feeding, while robins, chickadees, blue jays, and crows were rejoicing in the prolonged Indian summer, and bear and deer were not far off in the denser wood.

I came upon mother and son unexpectedly as I walked over the hills. The sound of sawing drew me down to a pretty growth of young pines. They were trimming up the trees. The mother would saw off the branches within her reach — which would not be very high up — and the taller, stronger sawyer would take the upper limbs. It was a picture one does not see every day. The beautiful trees will remember it as they spread out their arms to wider air and sunlight.

Another day I found them, one on each side of a fallen ash, which stroke by stroke they were cutting up into fireplace lengths with a great cross-cut saw, while the wind played through the gray locks of the one and over the curly pate of the other.

When next I saw them, they were far out on the lake in a canoe, each with a paddle, and I heard a cautious old man who was collecting eggs for the fish-hatcheries sing out to her, " Ain't ye afeard to be out in a canoe in winter? " and I heard her quick response, tinged with pride, " Not when I am with my son." The blue jay in the maple top shrieked with delight, and the fish-hawk swooping down for a black bass tumbled over himself with pleasure. They were *all* birds of one feather.

With a lantern to guide me down the stony path, though the full moon ought to have done it, I made bold to seek their cabin after the early shades of evening had fallen. A glorious fire roared up the chimney, before which the son was stretched out in creature comfort. A good light was on the rustic table, and in a low chair the mother was reading "Pickwick" aloud! No daily paper penetrated into their corner of the silent world.

The ten days' holiday must be over now, and mother and son again separated by weary miles, with the din of trolley cars and automobiles in their ears. Only a memory of the Indian summer remains, but it will remain long enough, perhaps, for the legend to be handed down to generations yet to come, that "papa and grandmamma went camping in winter, just by themselves, because he was so tied to her apron-strings."

* *Reprinted by courtesy of " The Outlook."*

MATER AMABILIS
By Emma Lazarus

Down the goldenest of streams,
    Tide of dreams,
The fair cradled man-child drifts:
Sways with the cadenced motion slow,
    To and fro,

As the mother-foot poised lightly, falls and
    lifts.

He, the firstling,— he, the light
    Of her sight,—
He, the breathing pledge of love,
'Neath the holy passion lies,
    Of her eyes,—
Smiles to feel the warm, life-giving ray above.

She believes that in his vision,
    Skies elysian
O'er an angel-people shine.
Back to gardens of delight,
    Taking flight,
His auroral spirit basks in dreams divine.

But she smiles through anxious tears;
    Unborn years
Pressing forward, she perceives.
Shadowy muffled shapes, they come
    Deaf and dumb,
Bringing what? dry chaff and tares, or full-
    eared sheaves?

What for him shall she invoke?
    Shall the oak
Bind the man's triumphant brow?
Shall his daring foot alight
    On the height?
Shall he dwell amidst the humble and the low?

Through what tears and sweat and pain,
    Must he gain
Fruitage from the tree of life?
Shall it yield him bitter flavor?
    Shall its savor
Be as manna midst the turmoil and the strife?

In his cradle slept and smiled
    Thus the child
Who as Prince of Peace was hailed.
Thus anigh the mother breast,
    Lulled to rest,
Child-Napoleon down the lilied river sailed.

Crowned or crucified — the same
    Glows the flame
Of her deathless love divine.
Still the blessed mother stands,
    In all lands,
As she watched beside thy cradle and by mine.

Whatso gifts the years bestow,
    Still men know,
While she breathes, lives one who sees
(Stand they pure or sin-defiled)
    But the child
Whom she crooned to sleep and rocked upon
        her knees.

TIRED MOTHERS

By May Riley Smith

A little elbow leans upon your knee,
  Your tired knee that has so much to bear;
A child's dear eyes are looking lovingly
  From underneath a thatch of tangled hair.
Perhaps you do not heed the velvet touch
  Of warm, moist fingers, folding yours so tight;
You do not prize this blessing overmuch,—
  You almost are too tired to pray to-night.

But it is blessedness! a year ago
  I did not see it as I do to-day —
We are so dull and thankless; and too slow
  To catch the sunshine till it slips away.
And now it seems surpassing strange to me,
  That, while I wore the badge of motherhood,
I did not kiss more oft and tenderly
  The little child that brought me only good.

And if some night when you sit down to rest,
  You miss this elbow from your tired knee,—
This restless curling head from off your breast,—
  This lisping tongue that chatters constantly;
If from your own the dimpled hands had slipped,
  And ne'er would nestle in your palm again;
If the white feet into the grave had tripped,
  I could not blame you for your heartache then.

I wonder so that mothers ever fret
　　At little children clinging to their gown;
Or that the footprints, when the days are wet,
　　Are ever black enough to make them frown.
If I could find a little muddy boot,
　　Or cap, or jacket, on my chamber floor,—
If I could kiss a rosy, restless foot,
　　And hear it patter in my house once more,—

If I could mend a broken cart to-day,
　　To-morrow make a kite to reach the sky,
There is no woman in God's world could say
　　She was more blissfully content than I.
But ah! the dainty pillow next my own
　　Is never rumpled by a shining head;
My singing birdling from its nest has flown,—
　　The little boy I used to kiss is dead!

GOING BLIND

By Ella Higginson

One time I heard a tender story told
　　About a mother who was going blind,
　　And ere the light went out forever, signed
Unto her children — while the sunset's gold
In burning ribbons down the West unrolled —
　　To gather close about, that she might trace
　　The lines upon each well-belovèd face,
That after — so I heard the story told —
Sun, moon, and stars and all dear things might fade,
　　And still their faces clearly be outlined

Against the golden background of that day.
Then came long night — but she was not afraid,
And ever answered —" Nay, I am not blind;
    My children's faces star my lonely way."
By permission of The Macmillan Company.

MOTHER AND SON

By Phœbe Cary

Brightly for him the future smiled,
    The world was all untried;
He had been a boy, almost a child,
    In your household till he died.

And you saw him young and strong and fair
    But yesterday depart;
And you now know he is lying there
    Shot to death through the heart!

Alas, for the step so proud and true
    That struck on the war-path's track;
Alas, to go, as he went from you,
    And to come, as they brought him back!

One shining curl from that bright young head,
    Held sacred in your home,
Is all that you have to keep in his stead
    In the years that are to come.

You may claim of his beauty and his youth
    Only this little part —
It is not much with which to stanch
    The wound in a mother's heart!

It is not much with which to dry
   The bitter tears that flow;
Not much in your empty hands to lie
   As the seasons come and go.

Yet he has not lived and died in vain,
   For proudly you may say
He has left a name without a stain
   For your tears to wash away.

And evermore shall your life be blest,
   Though your treasures now are few,
Since you gave for your country's good the best
   God ever gave to you!

THE MOTHER'S RETURN

By Dorothy Wordsworth

A month, sweet little ones, is past
Since your dear mother went away,—
And she to-morrow will return;
To-morrow is the happy day.

O blessed tidings! thought of joy!
The eldest heard with steady glee:
Silent he stood; then laughed amain,—
And shouted, " Mother, come to me!"

Louder and louder did he shout,
With witless hope to bring her near;

"Nay, patience! patience, little boy!
Your tender mother cannot hear."

I told of hills, and far-off towns,
And long, long vales to travel through; —
He listens, puzzled, sore perplexed,
But he submits; what can he do?

No strife disturbs his sister's breast;
She wars not with the mystery
Of time and distance, night and day;
The bonds of our humanity.

Her joy is like an instinct, joy
Of kitten, bird, or summer fly;
She dances, runs without an aim,
She chatters in her ecstasy.

Her brother now takes up the note,
And answers back his sister's glee:
They hug the infant in my arms,
As if to force his sympathy.

Then, settling into fond discourse,
We rested in the garden bower;
While sweetly shone the evening sun
In his departing hour.

We told o'er all that we had done,—
Our rambles by the swift brook's side
Far as the willow-skirted pool,
Where two fair swans together glide.

We talked of change, of winter gone,
Of green leaves on the hawthorn spray,
Of birds that build their nests and sing,
And all " since mother went away ! "

To her these tales they will repeat,
To her our new-born tribes will show,
The goslings green, the ass's colt,
The lambs that in the meadow go.

— But see, the evening star comes forth !
To bed the children must depart ;
A moment's heaviness they feel,
A sadness at the heart :

'Tis gone — and in a merry fit
They run up stairs in gamesome race ;
I, too, infected by their mood,
I could have joined the wanton chase.

Five minutes past — and, O the change !
Asleep upon their beds they lie ;
Their busy limbs in perfect rest,
And closed the sparkling eye.

SOME LITTLE LETTERS *

From Louisa M. Alcott: *Her Life, Letters and Journals.*

The Alcott children were required to keep their
journals regularly, and although these were open to

the inspection of father and mother, they were very frank, and really recorded their struggles and desires.

The Mother had the habit of writing little notes to the children when she wished to call their attention to any fault or peculiarity. Louisa preserved many of them, headed,—

(EXTRACTS from letters from Mother, received during these early years. I preserve them to show the ever tender, watchful help, she gave to the child who caused her the most anxiety, yet seemed to be the nearest to her heart till the end.— L. M. A.)

No. 1.— My Dear Little Girl,— Will you accept this doll from me on your seventh birthday? She will be a quiet playmate for my active Louisa for seven years more. Be a kind mamma, and love her for my sake.

Your Mother.

Beach Street, Boston, 1839.

FROM HER MOTHER

Cottage in Concord, 1842.

Dear Daughter,

Your tenth birthday has arrived. May it be a happy one, and on each returning birthday may you feel new strength and resolution to be gentle with sisters, obedient to parents, loving to every one, and happy in yourself.

I give you the pencil-case I promised, for I have

observed that you are fond of writing, and wish to encourage the habit.

Go on trying, dear, and each day it will be easier to be and do good. You must help yourself, for the cause of your little troubles is in yourself; and patience and courage only will make you what mother prays to see you,— her good and happy girl.

Concord, 1843.

DEAR LOUY,— I enclose a picture for you which I always liked very much, for I imagined that you might be just such an industrious daughter and I such a feeble but loving mother, looking to your labor for my daily bread.

Keep it for my sake and for your own, for you and I always liked to be grouped together.

MOTHER.

The lines I wrote under the picture in my journal: —

TO MOTHER

I hope that soon, dear mother,
  You and I may be
In the quiet room my fancy
  Has so often made for thee,—

The pleasant, sunny chamber,
  The cushioned easy-chair,
The book laid for your reading,
  The vase of flowers fair;

The desk beside the window,
  Where the sun shines warm and bright:
And there in ease and quiet
  The promised book you write;

While I sit close beside you,
  Content at last to see
That you can rest, dear mother,
  And I can cherish thee.

(The dream came true, and for the last ten years
of her life Marmee sat in peace, with every wish
granted, even to the " grouping together "; for she died
in my arms.— L. M. A.)

*Reprinted by permission of Little, Brown & Company, by whom
Miss Alcott's books are copyrighted.*

TWO MOTHERS

By Richard Burton

A woman walking the street adown
Saw at a casement, glint the gown
Of a mother, meek, whose little son
Had died with his child-joys just begun,
And it smote her heart, for well she knew
What Mother-love with a life may do;
And she said, " Poor soul! how sad that she
Should lose the child in his grace and glee!"
For she thought of *her* boy that lived to-day,
Though man-grown now and far away.

But the woman there in the window-seat
Looked with a smile, not sad, but sweet,

And touched with pity, to the place
Where she had marked the other's face;
And she said, " Poor soul! her child is lost,
For now he is only a man sin-tossed!
But the boy I watched in his bright young day,
He bides in my heart a child for aye."

MOTHER, NURSE, AND FAIRY

By John Gay

" Give me a son."   The blessing sent,
Were ever parents more content?
How partial are their doting eyes!
No child is half so fair and wise.

Waked to the morning's pleasing care,
The mother rose and sought her heir.
She saw the nurse like one possest,
With wringing hands and sobbing breast.
" Sure some disaster has befell:
" Speak Nurse: I hope the boy is well."
" Dear Madam, think not me to blame;
Invisible the Fairy came:
Your precious babe is hence conveyed,
And in the place a changling laid.
Where are the father's mouth and nose?
The mother's eyes, as black as sloes?
See here, a shocking arkward creature,
That speaks a fool in every feature."

" The woman 's blind, (the mother cries)
I see wit sparkle in his eyes."

" Lord, Madam, what a squinting leer!
No doubt the Fairy hath been here."
Just as she spoke, a pygmy sprite
Pops through the key hole swift as light;
Perched on the cradle's top he stands,
And thus her folly reprimands: —

" Whence sprung the vain conceited lie,
That we the world with fools supply?
What! give our sprightly race away
For the dull, helpless sons of clay!
Besides, by partial fondness shown,
Like you we dote upon our own.
Where yet was ever found a Mother
Who'd give her booby for another?
And should we change with human breed,
Well might we pass for fools indeed."

THE WIDOW'S MITE *

By Frederick Locker-Lampson

A Widow,— she had only one!
A puny and decrepit son;
   But, day and night,
Though fretful oft, and weak and small,
A loving child, he was her all,—
   The Widow's Mite.

The Widow's Mite — aye, so sustain'd,
She battled onward, nor complain'd

Though friends were fewer:
And while she toil'd for daily fare,
A little crutch upon the stair
  Was music to her.

I saw her then, and now I see
That, though resign'd and cheerful, she
  Has sorrow'd much:
She has,— He gave it tenderly,—
Much faith, and, carefully laid by,
  A little crutch.

* From " The Victorian Anthology." Houghton Mifflin Company.

CHILDREN

By Walter Savage Landor

Children are what the mothers are.
No fondest father's fondest care
Can fashion so the infant heart
As those creative beams that dart,
With all their hopes and fears, upon
The cradle of a sleeping son.

His startled eyes with wonder see
A father near him on his knee,
Who wishes all the while to trace
The mother in his future face;
But 'tis to her alone uprise
His waking arms; to her those eyes
Open with joy and not surprise.

WIDOW AND CHILD

By Alfred Tennyson

Home they brought her warrior dead;
    She nor swooned, nor uttered cry;
All her maidens, watching, said,
" She must weep or she will die."

Then they praised him soft and low,
    Called him worthy to be loved,
Truest friend and noblest foe;
    Yet she neither spoke nor moved.

Stole a maiden from her place,
    Lightly to the warrior stept,
Took a face-cloth from the face,
    Yet she neither moved nor wept.

Rose a nurse of ninety years,
    Set his child upon her knee —
Like summer tempest came her tears —
    " Sweet my child, I live for thee."

MOTHERS AND SONS *

By G. W. E. Russell

I know no pleasanter theme for contemplation than
this, and it is suggested to me by a letter from Ac-
crington. After referring to the qualities of the Man-
chester *Guardian,* my correspondent writes:

"I, a working woman, busy week in and week out, feel that I must find time to read its leaders; and some of them, written in stress and strain, are filed-up, in the hope that my sons may someday know how their mother treasured these things."

Who the mother is, who tries thus to influence her sons, I cannot tell, for the letter is anonymous; but I hope her lads recognize the fact that in this solicitude of a mother's love they possess one of the two richest boons which life can offer. If the other of those two boons is laid up for them in the storehouse of the unknown future, they are doubly blessed; but be that as it may, let them make the most of the blessing which they have for it will not last for ever.

> "He turned him right and round again,
>   Said 'Scorn na at my mither;
> Light loves I may get mony a ane,
>   But minnie ne'er anither.'"

It is my deliberate conviction that in one point at any rate — very likely in more — a poor boy's lot is happier than the lot of a boy born into what we call "the Upper Classes" and it is this — that the poor boy has so many more years of that inestimable blessing, a mother's watchful oversight. A mother's love and a mother's prayers may indeed follow their object round the world; but the personal intercourse and daily contact between mother and son have a sacramental virtue in guarding and shaping a boy's course such as nothing else on earth can supply. Every additional year spent at home, before the age of fourteen is reached, is a boon which cannot be over-estimated.

A man whose name would be perfectly well known to all my readers if I were at liberty to mention it has been heard to say: " It is more than thirty years since I lost my mother, but she still is to me an external conscience, pointing me in every exigency of life to the right path, and urging me to take it."

I fancy that the boys at Accrington, whose experience suggested this chapter, have a mother of that type; as they value their future peace, let them make the most of her while they have her.

There are foolish people in the world who imagine that from the pulpits of churches called " ritualistic " nothing is heard but formalism and dogma. No one could harbor this delusion who in the old days at St. Alban's Holborn, had heard Father Mackonochie insist, Good Friday after Good Friday, on the third word from the Cross — " Behold thy son: behold thy mother." I cannot for a moment doubt that those insistent warnings against unkindness, neglectfulness, and undutifulness helped to save many a mother's heart from breaking, and to cheer many a man's retrospect with the remembrance of a sacred duty loyally fulfilled. When Dean Farrar was a schoolmaster, it came to his knowledge that one of his favorite pupils was not as good a son to his mother as he might have been, and the kindly teacher drew thus upon his own experience: —

" My mother was, if ever there was, a Saint of God, and I loved her with all my heart; and yet one morning, when a letter brought me the intelligence that the previous night she had gone to bed in perfect health, and yet before morning God had called her to Himself — then my first thought was how much kinder, how much more loving I might have been; how in ten thousand ways by word and deed, which would have cost me nothing, and which would have caused her a thrill of happiness, I might have brightened her earthly life. It was a bitter thought that, much as I loved her, I had not always been so kind to her as I might have been; and I looked back with joy only to those occasions when I had *not* treated her love for me as a matter of course, but had shown, by acts of kindness and gentleness, how infinitely I valued her blessing and prayers."

There is, I think, no more impressive passage in biography than that which records the spiritual agonies of Monica as she wrestled against adversaries, seen and unseen, for the soul and future of the beloved but passion-driven Augustine. The art of Ary Scheffer has made visible to the eye the yearning of the mother's love, and the struggle with evil in the son's strong soul. It was Monica's hand that dragged Augustine out of the slough, and it was at Monica's feet that he poured out his contrition. Whenever, whether in Catholic or in Protestant theology, men feel the constraining spell of Augustine's teaching, let them give a thought to that long-tried and at length victorious mother who " lifted him out of the mire, and set him among princes."

If the modern Church has ever produced a saint, it was Edward King; and he was preëminently a mother's son.   To his under graduate-disciples at Oxford he would say: "Come and talk to my mother. She will do you more good than I can."   And after her death, he wrote: "How to get on, I don't quite see.   I am tempted to fear the loss of her wisdom almost more than the comfort of her brightness; but I know whence it came, and it can come still."

Those wistful words of a man past forty lend a pathetic interest to a letter which I have just received on the subject of Young Men's Melancholy.   "Do you not think that the loss of a good mother at an early age often results in this form of Melancholy? I attributed my state of mind in great part to such a loss when I was about thirteen."   Yes indeed! I think it, and I know it.   Of course, in what I have written so far, I have had in mind mothers who were not only tender but also wise.   Tenderness is indeed the sweetest ingredient in the spell which binds a lad to his mother; but "wisdom is profitable to direct," and not profitable only, but essential.   Monica once was over-tender to her son's worst faults; but experience taught her the wisdom of severity.   The foolish mother, whose blind idolatry fosters her boy's faults till they grow up into ruinous vices, was drawn for us by Dickens in Mrs. Steerforth.   George Eliot drew the wise mother — perhaps a little too completely wise — in Mrs. Garth.   Turning from fiction to actual life, we may see Mrs. Garth's substantial but unexciting virtues reproduced in the utterance which Matthew Arnold rather mischievously ridiculed as "Mrs. Gooch's Golden Rule."   "That beautiful sentence which Sir Daniel Gooch quoted to the Swindon work-men, and which I treasure as Mrs. Gooch's Golden Rule, or the Divine Injunction 'Be ye Perfect' done into British — the sentence which Sir Daniel Gooch's mother repeated to him every morning when he was a boy going to work: 'Ever remember, my dear Dan, that you should look forward to being some day Man-ager of that Concern.'"

To Matthew Arnold, with his mind set steadily on the things of the intellect and the spirit, the ideal thus bodied forth seemed inadequate. But I seem to recognize in it, through a medium of commonplace, that sedulous watchfulness of a mother's care, to which so many a man is heavily indebted for material suc-cess as well as for moral preservation. Anyhow, it is unwise and unsafe to disparage even the most homely manifestations of a mother's love for her son, or a son's love for his mother. Whether wisely or foolishly displayed, whether romantic or pedestrian in its as-pect and utterance, that mutual love is a passion which daily inspires heroic deeds, and, when brutally handled has before now culminated in the ghastliest tragedy. It is not so many years ago that two lads, maddened by the cruelties which their father was always inflict-ing on their mother, avenged her wrongs by parricide. With that crime, awful in itself and more awful in its consequences, I had, at the time, some personal concern. Many of my readers will remember it; and I only recall it now because it was one of those things which are "written for our admonition." I borrow my last word from Mr. James Rhoades —

O love of Son and Mother!
  New loves may wax and wane;
But shall we find another,
  Nor time nor tears can stain?
From life's august beginning,
  Through all her dark extremes —
Sole love that needs no winning
  Nor wastes in passionate dreams.

* *By permission of Grant Richards Company, Ltd.*

" MORE, PLEASE " *

By G. W. E. Russell

My chapter on " Mothers and Sons " has brought an
unusually wide and warm response.   I delight to think
that so fine a theme should have triumphed over de-
fects of handling, and should have touched exactly
those for whom the paper was written.   The words
at the head of this page are quoted from a postcard: —

                         Manchester, 10-8-12.
  I thought you had already reached the top, but to-
day's article crowns all.   *Deo Gratias.*   More, please.
— Yours to command,   A. B.

The subject is indeed inexhaustible and reaches far
and deep.   It has been said that there are only two
sorts of people in the world — men and women,— and
all relations between these two are cleansed and glori-
fied by the idea of motherhood.   This the Church of
Rome, with her fine sense of humanity, has recognized
in the Salutation, three times a day repeated from her

belfries — *Ave Maria, gratia plena; benedicta tu in mulieribus.*

It must have occurred to many of us, when gazing at Millet's wonderful picture of The Angelus, that English laborers and artisans might well envy his French peasants this reiterated reminder of the glory of motherhood and all that it imports. It was not a Catholic country — or, rather not in a Catholic province — but on the coast of Ulster, that one of the most brilliant and fascinating men of the Victorian age — statesman, orator, author, diplomatist, Proconsul,— the late Lord Dufferin, built a tower which commemorates his mother, the beautiful and famous Helen Sheridan; and Tennyson adorned it with one of his happiest inscriptions: —

> Helen's Tower, here I stand
> Dominant over sea and land.
> Son's love built me, and I hold
> Mother's love engrav'n in gold.
> Would my granite girth were strong
> As either love, to last as long!
> I should wear my crown entire.
> To and through the Doomsday fire,
> And be found of angel eyes
> In earth's recurring Paradise.

That tribute to the mutual love of Mother and Son, as a thing stronger and more durable than stone, has always seemed to me one of Tennyson's finest touches, and, by its ring of intense reality, it suggests that the poet no less than the statesman, was indeed a Mother's Son. A chivalric writer, depicting some young Crusader-Knights on a Syrian battlefield, just as the hosts of Heathendom were closing in for their destruction, described them as "buoyed up in that moment of surpassing peril by the sublime yet pathetic assurance that He for whom they gave their lives would receive their souls and comfort their Mothers." In all annals of battle, whether romantic or historical, the same thought perpetually recurs, till it finds its homeliest utterance in the words of the dying lad on the field of Belmont —"Tell Mother I'm sorry I ever laughed at her religion. I see now that she was right."

But I said just now that the idea of motherhood covers and sanctifies all human relations. A lad who has really loved his Mother (for love and reverence must go hand in hand) will instinctively regard all women as sisters for his Mother's sake. The one noble element in chivalry, in some respects so mischievous, was that it taught every aspirant to Knighthood that his first duty was to protect the weak, and to shield Womanhood from every touch or even breath of wrong. What Burke so gloriously said of Marie Antoinette — that "ten thousand swords must have leaped from their scabbards to avenge even a look that threatened her with insult"— should be true of every woman who lives in a country where the spirit of chivalry is not dead. She is surrounded by men and boys who have known a Mother's love and profited by it, and in each one of them she can claim a brother. Bishop King, who combined strength and gentleness in a singular harmony, thus advised a lad who sought his counsel:

" A very good rule is, never to say anything to a girl that you would not like another fellow to say to your sister. You know the word ' flirt.' Don't be one. It is unkind to a girl to be played with. Anyone who is a flirt will never be married happily. He will be despised. . . . Treat all those of the opposite sex as sisters; and from this treatment will not only follow repugnance and shame at personal action, but repugnance against others treating womankind not as sisters."

Here is the spirit of chivalry in a modern dress. The late Bishop Wilkinson of St. Andrews, who had ministered to Mr. Gladstone on his death-bed, made this striking allusion in his Funeral Sermon:

" I like to think of him in his young manhood, on that day when, in the presence of only one intimate friend, he solemnly made up his mind that, whatever else he accomplished in his life, whether he succeeded or whether he failed, he would by God's help not rest until he was able to bring back from the dreary wilderness some of those poor women whose lives had been ruined by man's selfishness, man's thoughtless cruelty. I like to see him as the young knight in the ancient legend, girding on his armor for that lifelong effort."

Chivalry again. But, though we are pledged soldiers for a great campaign, we need not always be fighting. Ours must be the attitude of the strong man armed, ready to strike a blow whenever the cause demands it; and our sisters will be all the readier to give us their friendship and their confidence because they know that we should be, if occasion arose, their champions. A

woman's perception of the chivalrous nature in man
— and its reverse — is the triumph of intuition.
Whatever is good in man, woman's influence draws
out and makes more gracious.   It was a famous say-
ing about a famous woman that " to have loved her
was a liberal education"; and the society of good
women is the most educative process through which a
man can pass.   It is not educative only, but disciplin-
ary.   A bumptious, or forward, or self-satisfied youth,
reminded by a word or even a look that he has gone too
far or made too free, has received a lesson by which,
if there is any good in him, he will profit to the end
of his days.   I said when I first touched on this sub-
ject, that the great drawback to the system of Board-
ing-Schools is that it withdraws a boy too soon from
his mother's care; and this might be added, that it
secludes him from women's society.   It deprives him
of those daily lessons in courtesy, chivalry, and self-
forgetfulness which the presence of women insensibly
impresses; and then as Gibbon says, outraged nature
will have her revenges.

"Home!   Sweet Home! " is still a possibility, and
a good home is the nursery of all virtues and all graces.
The goodness of a home is not dependent on wealth,
or spaciousness, or beauty, or luxury.   Everything de-
pends upon the Mother.   Her love is a sacramental
benediction, and her watchfulness a spell which Satan
fears.   The Prophet of old time, when he desired to
heal the noxious stream, " went forth unto the spring
of waters, and cast the salt in there."   A Mother's
influence on the home is the salt cast in at the spring

of the waters. "There shall not be from thence any more death or barren land." From a good home, thankfully and reverently used, flows the stream of a good, a pure, and a profitable life.

* By permission of Grant Richards Company, Ltd.

MEPHIBOSHETH

BY NATHANIEL P. WILLIS

As if he were a vision that would fade,
Rizpah gazed on him. Never, to her eye,
Grew his bright form familiar; but, like stars,
That seem'd each night new lit in a new heaven,
He was each morn's sweet gift to her. She loved
Her first-born, as a mother loves her child,
Tenderly, fondly. But for him — the last —
What had she done for heaven to be his mother!
Her heart rose in her throat to hear his voice;
She look'd on him forever through her tears;
Her utterance, when she spoke to him, sank down,
As if the lightest thought of him had lain
In an unfathom'd cavern of her soul.
The morning light was part of him, to her —
What broke the day for, but to show his beauty?
The hours but measured time till he should come;
Too tardy sang the bird when he was gone;
She would have shut the flowers — and call'd the star
Back to the mountain-top — and bade the sun
Pause at eve's golden door — to wait for him!
Was this a heart gone wild? — or is the love

Of mothers like a madness? Such as this
Is many a poor one in her humble home,
Who silently and sweetly sits alone,
Pouring her life all out upon her child.
What cares she that he does not feel how close
Her heart beats after his — that all unseen
Are the fond thoughts that follow him by day,
And watch his sleep like angels? And, when moved
By some sore needed Providence, he stops
In his wild path and lifts a thought to heaven,
What cares the mother that he does not see
The link between the blessing and her prayer!

THE MOURNING MOTHER

(OF THE DEAD BLIND)

BY ELIZABETH BARRETT BROWNING

Dost thou weep, mourning mother,
  For thy blind boy in the grave?
That no more with each other,
  Sweet counsel ye can have? —
That he, left dark by nature,
  Can never more be led
By thee, maternal creature,
  Along smooth paths instead?
That thou canst no more show him
  The sunshine, by the heat:
The river's silver flowing,
  By murmurs at his feet?

The foliage by its coolness;
  The roses, by their smell;
And all creation's fulness,
  By Love's invisible?
Weepest thou to behold not
  His meek blind eyes again,—
Closed doorways which were folded,
  And prayed against in vain —
And under which, sate smiling
  The child-mouth evermore,
As one who watcheth, wiling
  The time by, at the door?
And weepest thou to feel not
  His clinging hand in thine —
Which now, at dream-time, will not
  Its cold touch disentwine?
And weepest thou still ofter,
  Oh, never more to mark
His low soft words, made softer
  By speaking in the dark?
Weep on, thou mourning mother!

II

But since to him when living
  Thou wast both sun and moon,
Look o'er his grave, surviving
  From a high sphere alone.
Sustain that exaltation,
  Expand that tender light,
And hold in mother-passion
  Thy Blessèd in thy sight.

See how he went out straightway
   From the dark world he knew,—
No twilight in the gateway
   To mediate 'twixt two,—
Into the sudden glory,
   Out of the dark he trod,
Departing from before thee
   At once to light and God! —
For the first face, beholding
   The Christ's in its divine,
For the first place, the golden
   And tideless hyaline;
With trees, as lasting summer,
   That rock to songful sound,
While angels, the new-comer,
   Wrap a still smile around.
Oh, in the blessed psalm now,
   His happy voice he tries,
Spreading a thicker palm-bough,
   Than others o'er his eyes!
Yet still, in all the singing,
   Thinks haply of thy song
Which, in his life's first springing,
   Sang to him all night long;
And wishes it beside him,
   With kissing lips that cool
And soft did overglide him,
   To make the sweetness full.
Look up, O mourning mother,
   Thy blind boy walks in light!
Ye wait for one another,

Before God's infinite.
But thou art now the darkest,
  Thou mother left below —
Thou, the sole blind,— thou markest,
  Content that it be so,—
Until ye two have meeting
  Where Heaven's pearl gate is,
And *he* shall lead thy feet in,
  As once thou leddest *his*.
Wait on, thou mourning mother.

NIOBE *

By Alfred Noyes

How like the sky she bends above her child,
  One with the great horizon of her pain!
No sob from our low seas where woe runs wild,
  No weeping cloud, no momentary rain,
Can mar the heaven-high visage of her grief,
  That frozen anguish, proud, majestic, dumb.
    She stoops in pity above the laboring earth,
      Knowing how fond, how brief
  Is all its hope, past, present, and to come,
    She stoops in pity, and yearns to assuage its
      dearth.

Through that fair face the whole dark universe
  Speaks, as a thorn-tree speaks thro' one white
      flower;
And all those wrenched Promethean souls that curse
  The gods, but cannot die before their hour,

Find utterance in her beauty. That fair head
　　Bows over all earth's graves. It was her cry
　　　Men heard in Rama when the twisted ways
With children's blood ran red!
　　Her silence utters all the sea would sigh;
　　　And, in her face, the whole earth's anguish prays.

It is the pity, the pity of human love
　　That strains her face, upturned to meet the doom,
And her deep bosom, like a snow-white dove
　　Frozen upon its nest, ne'er to resume
Its happy breathing o'er the golden brace
　　Whose fostering was her death. Death, death alone
　　　Can break the anguished horror of that spell!
The sorrow on her face
　　Is sealed: the living flesh is turned to stone;
　　　She knows all, all, that Life and Time can tell.

Ah, yet, her woman's love, so vast, so tender;
　　Her woman's body, hurt by every dart;
Braving the thunder, still, still hide the slender
　　Soft frightened child beneath her mighty heart!
She is all one mute immortal cry, one brief
　　Infinite pang of such victorious pain
　　　That she transcends the heavens and bows them
　　　　down!
The majesty of grief
　　Is hers, and her dominion must remain
　　　Eternal. God nor man usurps that crown.

* From " The Golden Hynde," published by The Macmillan Company.

THE MOTHER

TRANSLATED FROM THE CHINESE BY GEORGE BARROW

From out the South the genial breezes sigh,
They shake the bramble branches to and fro
Whose lovely green delights the gazer's eye:
A mother's thoughts are troubled even so.

From out the South the genial breezes move,
They shake the branches of the bramble tree:
Unless the sons fair men and honest prove,
The virtuous mother will dishonored be.

The frigid fount with violence and spray
By Shiyoun's town upcasts its watery store:
Though full seven sons she gave to life and day,
The mother's heart is but disturbed the more.

When sings the redbreast, it is bliss to hear,
The dulcet notes the little songster breeds;
But ah! more blissful to a mother's ear,
The fair report of seven good children's deeds.

A MOTHER'S LOVE — HOME

BY ALBERT BARNES

Many of us — most of us who are advanced beyond
the period of childhood — went out from that home to
embark on the stormy sea of life. Of the feelings of
a father, and of his interest in our welfare, we have

never entertained a doubt, and our home was dear because he was there; but there was a peculiarity in the feeling that it was the home of our mother. While she lived there, there was a place that we felt was *home*. There was one place where we would always be welcome, one place where we would be met with a smile, one place where we would be sure of a friend. The world might be indifferent to us. We might be unsuccessful in our studies or our business. The new friends which we supposed we had might prove to be false. The honor which we thought we deserved might be withheld from us. We might be chagrined and mortified by seeing a rival outstrip us, and bear away the prize which we sought. But there was a place where no feelings of rivalry were found, and where those whom the world overlooked would be sure of a friendly greeting. Whether pale or wan by study, care, or sickness, or flushed with health and flattering success, we were sure we should be welcomed there. Though the world was cold towards us, yet there was one who always rejoiced in our success, and always was affected by our reverses; and there was a place to which we might go back from the storm which began to pelt us, where we might rest, and become encouraged and invigorated for a new conflict. So I have seen a bird in its first efforts to fly, leave its nest, and stretch its wings, and go forth to the wide world. But the wind blew it back, and the rain began to fall, and the darkness of night began to draw on, and there was no shelter abroad, and it sought its way back to its nest, to take shelter beneath its mother's wings, and be refreshed for the struggles of a new day; but then it flew away to think of its nest and its mother no more. But not thus did we leave our home when we bade adieu to it to go forth alone to the manly duties of life. Even amidst the storms that then beat upon us, and the disappointments that we met with, and the coldness of the world, we felt still that there was one there who sympathized in our troubles, as well as rejoiced in our success, and that, whatever might be abroad, when we entered her dwelling we should be met with a smile. We expected that a mother, like the mother of Sisera, as she "looked out at her window," waiting for the coming of her son laden with the spoils of victory, would look out for *our* coming, and that our return would renew her joy and ours in our earlier days.

It makes a sad desolation when from such a place a mother is taken away, and when, whatever may be the sorrows or the successes in life, she is to greet the returning son or daughter no more. The home of our childhood may be still lovely. The old family mansion — the green fields — the running stream — the moss-covered well — the trees — the lawn — the rose — the sweet briar — may be there. Perchance, too, there may be an aged father, with venerable locks, sitting in his loneliness, with everything to command respect and love; but she is not there. Her familiar voice is not heard. The mother has been borne forth to sleep by the side of her children who went before her, and the place is not what it was. There may be those there whom we much love, but she is not there.

We may have formed new relations in life, tender and strong as they can be; we may have another home, dear to us as was the home of our childhood, where there is all in affection, kindness, and religion, to make us happy, but *that* home is not what it was, and it never will be what it was again.   It is a loosening of one of the cords which bound us to earth, designed to prepare us for our eternal flight from everything dear here below, and to teach us that there is *no* place here that is to be our permanent home.

THE SONG OF THE OLD MOTHER *

BY WILLIAM BUTLER YEATS

I rise in the dawn, and I kneel and I blow
Till the seed of the fire flicker and glow,
And then I must scrub, and bake, and sweep,
Till stars are beginning to blink and peep;
But the young lie long and dream in their bed
Of matching of ribbons, the blue and the red,
And their day goes over in idleness,
And they sigh if the wind but lift up a tress;
While I must work, because I am old
And the seed of the fire gets feeble and cold.

* *From " The Victorian Anthology."*

MOTHER AND POET

BY ELIZABETH BARRETT BROWNING

Dead!   One of them shot by the sea in the east,
And one of them shot in the west by the sea.

Dead! both my boys! When you sit at the feast
  And are wanting a great song for Italy free,
  Let none look at *me!*

Yet I was a poetess only last year,
  And good at my art, for a woman men said;
But *this* woman, *this,* who is agoniz'd here,
  — The east sea and west sea rhyme on in her head
  Forever instead.

What art can a woman be good at? Oh, vain!
  What art *is* she good at, but hurting her breast
With the milk-teeth of babes, and a smile at the pain?
  Ah boys, how you hurt! you were strong as you
      pressed
  And I proud, by that test.

What art's for a woman? To hold on her knees
  Both darlings; to feel all their arms round her throat,
Cling, strangle a little, to sew by degrees
  And 'broider the long-clothes and neat little coat;
  To dream and to doat.

To teach them . . . It stings there! I made them in-
      deed
  Speak plain the word *country.* I taught them, no
      doubt,
That a country's a thing men should die for at need.
  I prated of liberty, rights, and about
  The tyrant cast out.

And when their eyes flashed . . . O my beautiful
    eyes ! . . .
  I exulted; nay, let them go forth at the wheels
Of the guns, and denied not.   But then the surprise
  When one sits quite alone!   Then one weeps, then
    one kneels!
  God, how the house feels!

At first, happy news came, in gay letters moil'd
  With my kisses,— of camp-life and glory, and how
They both lov'd me; and, soon coming home to be
    spoil'd,
  In return would fan off every fly from my brow
  With their green laurel-bough.

Then was triumph at Turin: " Ancona was free! "
  And some one came out of the cheers in the street,
With a face pale as stone, to say something to me.
  My Guido was dead!   I fell down at his feet,
  While they cheer'd in the street.

I bore it; friends sooth'd me; my grief look'd sublime
  As the ransom of Italy.   One boy remain'd
To be leant on and walk'd with, recalling the time
  When the first grew immortal, while both of
    them strain'd
  To the height he had gain'd.

And letters still came, shorter, sadder, more strong,
  Writ now but in one hand, " I was not to faint,—

One lov'd me for two — would be with me ere long:
  And *Viva l'Italia!* — *he* died for, our saint,
  Who forbids our complaint."

My Nanni would add, " he was safe, and aware
  Of a presence that turn'd off the balls,— was im-
     press'd
It was Guido himself, who knew what I could bear,
  And how 'twas impossible, quite dispossess'd,
  To live on for the rest."

On which without pause, up the telegraph-line,
  Swept smoothly the next news from Gaeta: — *Shot.*
Tell his mother. Ah, ah, " his," " their" mother,—
     not " mine,"
  No voice says *" My* mother " again to me. What!
  You think Guido forgot?

Are souls straight so happy that, dizzy with Heaven,
  They drop earth's affections, conceive not of woe?
I think not. Themselves were too lately forgiven
  Through that Love and Sorrow which reconcil'd so
  The Above and Below.

O Christ of the five wounds, who look'st through the
     dark
  To the face of Thy Mother! consider I pray,
How we common mothers stand desolate, mark,
  Whose sons, not being Christs, die with eyes turn'd
     away,
  And no last word to say!

Both boys dead? but that's out of nature.   We all
  Have been patriots, yet each house must always
     keep one.
'Twere imbecile, hewing out roads to a wall;
  And, when Italy's made, for what end is it done
  If we have not a son?

Ah, ah, ah! when Gaeta's taken, what then?
  When the fair wicked queen sits no more at her
     sport
Of the fire-balls of death crashing souls out of men?
  When the guns of Cavalli with final retort
  Have cut the game short?

When Venice and Rome keep their new jubilee,
  When your flag takes all heaven for its white, green,
     and red,
When *you* have your country from mountain to sea,
  When King Victor has Italy's crown on his head,
  (And I have my Dead) —

What then?   Do not mock me.   Ah, ring your bells
     low,
  And burn your lights faintly! *My* country is
     there,
Above the star prick'd by the last peak of snow:
  My Italy's *there,* with my brave civic Pair,
  To disfranchise despair!

Forgive me.   Some women bear children in strength,
  And bite back the cry of their pain in self-scorn;

But the birth-pangs of nations will wring us at length
  Into wail such as this — and we sit on forlorn
When the man-child is born.

Dead! One of them shot by the sea in the east,
  And one of them shot in the west by the sea,
Both! both my boys! If in keeping the feast,
  You want a great song for your Italy free,
  Let none look at *me*.

"MOTHER," AND "MOTHER CAREY'S CHICKENS."

A Review from *The Outlook*

. . . The young girls and older women who have
adopted the habits, dress, and moral standards of the
fast set are, happily, a very small minority, but the
signs of their increase in numbers are very disconcert-
ing. It is a great relief, in this widening morass of
lowered standards, cheapened and superficial ideals
of life, and love of vulgar publicity, to come upon
simple, wholesome, fundamental stories which deal
reverently with the vital things of life. Such a story
of Mrs. Norris's "Mother" after half a dozen novels
of the emancipated kind, gives one a sense of escape
from fetid air into mountain air, from a casino into a
home. It is a very simple story, and for that reason
those who require highly seasoned fiction whose chief
figures are irresponsible men seeking "soul unions"
and feather-brained women skirting the edges of the

great disaster will class it as archaic and outgrown; as a matter of fact, it is one of the really fundamental stories of the season. The OUTLOOK has already summarized its simple plot: a young girl taken from a pinched and crowded home full of love and devotion into an atmosphere of luxury, idleness, overfeeding, over-drinking, over-dressing, and nervous endeavor to be free by escaping from the care of children, the responsibility of the home, and going back to the old familiar ties which, since society began to be civilized, have bound men and women alike to duty, honor, and unselfishness, and to the searching and redeeming education of work and service and self-denial, which have been rejected and cast aside as outworn whenever society has reverted to the barbarism of physical ease and spiritual poverty.

The author of "Mother" has not written from a place of shelter; she has made her own way and has learned in the school of life those primary lessons which, like the old-fashioned drill in reading, writing and arithmetic, train the mind for the freedom that comes through strength. She has been a bookkeeper, librarian, settlement worker, and reporter, as well as a wife and mother; and has therefore seen life from many sides. She has kept a clear sense of values, a sane view of the supreme things, a resolute grip on the fundamental realities. The rush for freedom has not taken her off her feet; nor has the moral confusion through which society is passing, on its road to that real freedom which is based on self-denial, subordination of self, and a clear, joyful acceptance of duty, blinded her. "Mother" is a story of a girl who was saved from the shipwreck of mistaking luxury for happiness and escape from duty for freedom; in pleasure-loving America, with its increasing class of women of leisure, such a story, in a quiet way, has a real service to render.

And so has Mrs. Riggs's "Mother Carey's Chickens" a story of real boys and girls with a real mother, who faces a great crisis in the life of her little family with saving good sense and with the courage that is half the battle. There is no high tragedy in the retreat of a fatherless family into the country, no dramatic staging of the fight with poverty; there are loyal affection, clear perception of real values, plenty of humor, and that wholesomeness of tone and spirit which breed health, courage, and character.

These two unpretentious stories are good examples of the kind of reading which serves as an anti-toxin at a time when many demoralizing, relaxing, enervating stories are in the hands of young girls who know nothing about life, and are in danger of losing their footing on those fundamental principles sometimes covered with foam and spume, but never moved from their indestructible bases. In a time in which there is a wide and inspiring movement toward real freedom there are many who are in danger of falling victims to a false idea of freedom, only to find when it is too late that, instead of escaping from bondage to reality into a beautiful idealism, they have flung themselves against immutable laws, and the drama of emancipation has turned into cheap farce or pitiful tragedy.

If a record could be kept of the " affinities " and " soul unions " reported by the newspapers and of their results five years later, the tinsel romance would turn to tawdry melodrama.

MATERNAL GRIEF

By William Wordsworth

Departed Child! I could forget thee once
Though at my bosom nursed; this woeful gain
Thy dissolution brings, that in my soul
Is present and perpetually abides
A shadow, never, never to be displaced
By the returning substance, seen or touched,
Seen by my eyes, or clasped in my embrace.
Absence and death how differ they! and how
Shall I admit that nothing can restore
What one short sigh so easily removed? —
Death, life, and sleep, reality and thought,
Assist me, God, their boundaries to know,
O teach me calm submission to thy Will!

The Child she mourned had overstepped the pale
Of Infancy, but still did breathe the air
That sanctifies its confines, and partook
Reflected beams of that celestial light
To all the Little-ones on sinful earth
Not unvouchsafed — a light that warmed and cheered
Those several qualities of heart and mind
Which, in her own blest nature, rooted deep,

Daily before the Mother's watchful eye,
And not hers only, their peculiar charms
Unfolded,— beauty, for its present self,
And for its promises to future years,
With not unfrequent rapture fondly hailed.

Have you espied upon a dewy lawn
A pair of Leverets each provoking each
To a continuance of their fearless sport,
Two separate Creatures in their several gifts
Abounding, but so fashioned that, in all
That Nature prompts them to display, their looks,
Their starts of motion and their fits of rest,
An undistinguishable style appears
And character of gladness, as if Spring
Lodged in their innocent bosoms, and the spirit
Of rejoicing morning were their own?

Such union, in the lovely Girl maintained
And her twin Brother, had the parent seen
Ere, pouncing like a ravenous bird of prey,
Death in a moment parted them, and left
The Mother, in her turns of anguish, worse
Than desolate; for oft-times from the sound
Of the survivor's sweetest voice (dear child,
He knew it not) and from his happiest looks
Did she extract the food of self-reproach,
As one that lived ungrateful for the stay
By Heaven afforded to uphold her maimed
And tottering spirit.   And full off the Boy,

Now first acquainted with distress and grief,
Shrunk from his Mother's presence, shunned with fear
Her sad approach, and stole away to find,
In his known haunts of joy where'er he might,
A more congenial object.   But, as time
Softened her pangs and reconciled the child
To what he saw, he gradually returned,
Like a scared Bird encouraged to renew
A broken intercourse; and, while his eyes
Were yet with pensive fear and gentle awe
Turned upon her who bore him, she would stoop
To imprint a kiss that lacked not power to spread
Faint color over both their pallid cheeks,
And stilled his tremulous lip.   Thus they were calmed
And cheered; and now together breathe fresh air
In open fields; and when the glare of day
Is gone, and twilight to the Mother's wish
Befriends the observance, readily they join
In walks whose boundary is the lost One's grave,
Which he with flowers had planted, finding there
Amusement, where the Mother does not miss
Dear consolation, kneeling on the turf
In prayer, yet blending with that solemn rite
Of pious faith the vanities of grief;
For such, by pitying Angels and by Spirits
Transferred to regions upon which the clouds
Of our weak nature rest not, must be deemed
Those willing tears, and unforbidden sighs,
And all those tokens of a cherished sorrow,
Which, soothed and sweetened by the grace of Heaven

As now it is, seems to her own fond heart,
Immortal as the love that gave it being.

MOTHER AND HOME

By John Jarvis Holden

Mother! Home! — that blest refrain
   Sounds through every hastening year:
All things go, but these remain.

Held in memory's jeweled chain,
   Names most precious, names thrice dear:
Mother! Home! — that blest refrain.

How it sings away my pain!
   How it stills my waking fear!
All things go, but these remain.

Griefs may grow and sorrows wane,
   E'er that melody I hear:
Mother! Home! — that blest refrain.

Tenderness in every strain,
   Thoughts to worship and revere:
All things go, but these remain.

Every night you smile again,
   Every day you bring me cheer:
Mother! Home! — that blest refrain:
   All things go, but these remain!

FROM THE DREAM

By Mrs. Norton

Sweet is the image of the brooding dove! —
Holy as Heaven a mother's tender love!
The love of many prayers and many tears,
Which changes not with dim declining years —
The only love which on this teeming earth
Asks no return from Passion's wayward birth;
The only love that, with a touch divine,
Displaces from the heart's most secret shrine
The idol Self.   Oh! prized beneath thy due
When life's untried affections all are new —
Love, from whose calmer hope and holier rest
(Like a fledged bird, impatient of the nest)
The human heart, rebellious, springs to seek
Delights more vehement, in ties more weak;
How strange to us appears, in after-life,
That term of mingled carelessness and strife,
When guardianship so gentle gall'd our pride,
When it was holiday to leave thy side,
When, with dull ignorance that would not learn,
We lost those hours that never can return —
Hours, whose most sweet communion Nature meant
Should be in confidence and kindness spent,
That we (hereafter mourning) might believe
In human faith, though all around deceive;
Might weigh against the sad and startling crowd
Of ills which wound the weak and chill the proud,
Of woes 'neath which (despite of stubborn will,
Philosophy's vain boast, and erring skill)

The strong heart downward like a willow bends,
Failure of love,— and treachery of friends,—
Our recollections of the undefiled,
The sainted tie, of parent and of child!
Oh! happy days! Oh, years that glided by,
Scarce chronicled by one poor passing sigh!
When the dark storm sweeps past us, and the soul
Struggles with fainting strength to reach the goal;
When the false baits that lured us only cloy,
What would we give to grasp your vanish'd joy!
From the cold quicksands of Life's treacherous shore
The backward light our anxious eyes explore,
Measure the miles our wandering feet have come,
Sinking heart-weary, far away from home,
Recall the voice that whisper'd love and peace
The smile that bid our early sorrows cease,
And long to bow our grieving heads, and weep
Low on the gentle breast that lull'd us first to sleep!

Ah! bless'd are they for whom 'mid all their pains
That faithful and unalter'd love remains;
Who, Life wreck'd round them — hunted from their
    rest,—
And by all else forsaken or distress'd,—
Claim, in one heart, their sanctuary and shrine —
As, I, my Mother, claim'd my place in thine!

MY MOTHER

By Josephine Rice Creelman

I walk upon the rocky shore,
Her strength is in the ocean's roar.

I glance into the shaded pool,
Her mind is there so calm and cool.
I hear sweet rippling of the sea,
Naught but her laughter 'tis to me.
I gaze into the starry skies,
And there I see her wondrous eyes.
I look into my inmost mind,
And here her inspiration find.
In all I am and hear and see,
My precious mother is with me.

SEVEN TIMES FOUR. MATERNITY

By Jean Ingelow

From Songs of Seven

Heigh ho! daisies and buttercups,
  Fair yellow daffodils, stately and tall,
When the wind wakes how they rock in the grasses,
  And dance with the cuckoo-buds, slender and small:
Here's two bonny boys, and here's mother's own lasses,
  Eager to gather them all.

Heigh ho! daisies and buttercups,
  Mother shall thread them a daisy chain;
Sing them a song of the pretty hedge-sparrow,
  That loved her brown little ones, loved them full
      fain;

Sing, " Heart thou art wide though the house be but
    narrow "—
  Sing once, and sing it again.

Heigh ho! daisies and buttercups,
  Sweet wagging cowslips, they bend and they bow;
A ship sails afar over warm ocean waters,
  And haply one musing doth stand at her prow.
O bonny brown sons, and O sweet little daughters,
  Maybe he thinks on you now!

Heigh ho! daisies and buttercups,
  Fair yellow daffodils stately and tall;
A sunshiny world full of laughter and leisure,
  And fresh hearts unconscious of sorrow and thrall,
Send down on their pleasure smiles passing its
    measure —
  God that is over us all.

SEVEN TIMES SEVEN. LONGING FOR HOME

By Jean Ingelow

From Songs of Seven

I

A song of a boat: —
There was once a boat on a billow:
Lightly she rocked to her port remote,
And the foam was white in her wake like snow,

And her frail mast bowed when the breeze would blow,
  And bent like a wand of willow.

II

I shaded mine eyes one day when a boat
  Went courtesying over the billow,
I marked her course till a dancing mote
She faded out on the moonlit foam,
And I stayed behind in the dear loved home;
  And my thoughts all day were about a boat,
    And my dreams upon the pillow.

III

I pray you hear my song of a boat,
  For it is but short: —
My boat, you shall find none fairer afloat,
  In river or port.
Long I looked out for the lad she bore,
  On the open desolate sea,
And I think he sailed to the heavenly shore,
  For he came not back to me —
            Ah me!

IV

A song of a nest: —
There was once a nest in a hollow,
Down in the mosses and knot-grass pressed,
  Soft and warm, and full to the brim;
  Vetches leaned over it purple and dim,
    With buttercup buds to follow.

V

I pray you hear my song of a nest,
 For it is not long: —
You shall never light in a summer quest
 The bushes among —
Shall never light on a prouder sitter,
 A fairer nestful, nor ever know
A softer sound than their twitter,
 That wind-like did come and go.

VI

I had a nestful of my own,
 Ah happy, happy I!
Right dearly I loved them; but when they were grown
 They spread out their wings to fly —
O, one after one they flew away
 Far up to the heavenly blue,
To the better country, the upper day,
 And — I wish I was going too.

VII

I pray you, what is the nest to me,
 My empty nest?
And what is the shore where I stood to see
 My boat sail down to the west?
Can I call that home where I anchor yet,
 Though my good man has sailed?
Can I call that home where my nest was set,
 Now all its hope hath failed?

Nay, but the port where my sailor went,
    And the land where my nestlings be:
There is the home where my thoughts are sent,
    The only home for me —
            Ah me!

VI

MOTHERS OF THE FAMOUS

THE MOTHER OF ABRAHAM LINCOLN *

By Ida M. Tarbell

Abraham Lincoln, born in Kentucky, was descended from New England ancestry, from which he inherited an intense love of liberty, thoroughness of character and perfect integrity. As often happens, these qualities did not appear in his father, who was poor, improvident and ignorant. His mother was an energetic Christian woman of much refinement whose devotion to her domestic and maternal duties soon wore out her frail body, but imprinted her image indelibly on the heart of her son. Many times he said that all he was he owed to her. Then it must be assumed that to her he owed his rugged honesty, which became part of his name, and that thoroughness which led him to commit much of the Bible to memory, and which lay at the foundation of his success.

Tradition has it that Mrs. Lincoln took great pains to teach her children what she knew, and that at her knee they heard all the Bible lore, fairy tales, and country legends that she had been able to gather in her poor life.

Lincoln's life had its tragedies as well as its touch of romance — tragedies so real and profound that they gave dignity to all the crudeness and poverty which surrounded him, and quickened and intensified the melancholy temperament which he inherited from his mother. Away back in 1816 when Thomas Lincoln had started to find a farm in Indiana, bidding his wife be ready to go into the wilderness on his return, Nancy Lincoln had taken her boy and her girl to a tiny grave, that of her youngest child: and the three had there said good-by to a little one whom the children had scarcely known, but for whom the mother's grief was so keen that the boy never forgot the scene.

Two years later he saw his father make a green pine box and put his dead mother into it, and he saw her buried not far from their cabin, without a prayer. Young as he was, it was his efforts, it is said, which brought a parson from Kentucky, three months later, to preach the sermon and conduct the service which seemed to the child a necessary honor to the dead.

From the Publications of the Lincoln History Society.

MOTHERS OF THE GREAT

By Grace Greenwood

I have been reading Lamartine. I have finished "Raphael," and am almost through the "Memoires." Need I say that I am enchanted with both? The "Raphael" is a pure love-poem in the form of prose, indeed, but a poem in essence. Some think the story an exaggeration, if not an utter impossibility. I do not so esteem it. It is the ideal of a pure, unselfish love, with the depth and eternity of a great passion, without sensuality and without satiety. Its glow and strength and glory are not borrowed from poetry, but are of its own nature, where it existed in all its intensity and infinity in the spirit of genius. Every true poet possesses a realm of perpetual summer, of more than tropical bloom and luxuriance, in its own being — an Italy of the soul; and this is only thrown open to us, truthfully revealed in Raphael.

But this work impresses the sensibilities and captivates the imagination — the " Memoires " come home to the heart. We there love, we enjoy, we feel intensely the artless ways, the innocent pleasures, the touching trials of childhood — we are carried back to that fresh, glowing season — we live in it again, with all its tenderness and truth, its laughter and tears, its harmony with nature, and its nearness to God.

It is curious to remark how Lamartine has made this entire work little more than a grand memorial, an immortalization, an apotheosis of his adored mother.

And to me it seems that it is this sentiment of filial piety, this first, purest, holiest flower of the heart, yet fresh with its morning dew, yet sweet with its early fragrance, yet unwithered by the noontide blaze of fame, and unblighted by the cares of the world or the frosts of time, which more than his genius or his patriotism, constitutes the peculiar beauty and glory of Lamartine's character.

To the benign influence of his mother, and to his having breathed such an atmosphere of tenderness in his childhood, we may ascribe not only the piety of this noble poet, but the strong infusion of the woman observable in his nature.

But it is of the high-souled, the heroic, the Christian

woman — one not wrapt in visions, and revelations, and ecstasies — walking on clouds and gazing longingly toward heaven — but one whose heaven is within and around her — looking from her eyes, breathing from her lips, eloquent in her life, and triumphant in her faith.

Again, I say, how *beautiful* is Lamartine's love for his mother! More beautiful even in its heart-warmth, its tender, impassioned worship than that deep love which prevailed with the stern Roman, against the hot sense of wrong, and "allayed his rages and revenges" when the noble Volumnia prayed.

How striking and complete is the contrast between Lamartine and Byron, and how much of this difference may have been owing to early domestic influences.

"*Heaven* lies about us in our infancy," the one might say; the other would have substituted quite another word for the "heaven." Byron, almost from the first, was shut out from the love and holiness of the divine life which is the native home of the spirit; but Lamartine was ever drawn toward it, bound to it as with golden chains, by the gentle piety and angelic tenderness of that pure, maternal heart. Her faith has been the anchor of his soul — her memory is as a shape of hope and peace, which ever sits smiling at the helm of his life-barque; but Byron floated forth alone, on a wild, unfriendly sea, with no "sweet spirit" to cheer and console, and no hand to save, when the storm came down, and the deep waters passed over him.

Byron's mother! — what arms were hers to receive the mortal incarnation of that beautiful and terrible genius — what a bosom was hers to pillow that head, molded like a Grecian god's, but destined to be crowned with a grander immortality — what a spirit to guide that passion-freighted heart, that will of iron, and that soul of fire! What wonder that the sunlight of love shone but faintly and at intervals on that troubled life. The morning was darkened, the hot noon soon overcast, and the night closed in early, with gloom and tempest.

REGINA COELI

By Coventry Patmore

Say, did his sisters wonder what could
      Joseph see
In a mild, silent little Maid like thee?
And was it awful in that narrow house,
With God for Babe and Spouse?
Nay, like thy simple, female sort, each one
Apt to find Him in Husband and in Son,
Nothing to thee came strange in this.
Thy wonder was but wondrous bliss:
Wondrous, for, though
True Virgin lives not but does know,
(Howbeit none ever yet confess'd)
That God lies really in her breast,
Of thine He made His special nest!
And so
All mothers worship little feet,
And kiss the very ground they've trod;

But, ah, thy little Baby sweet
Who was indeed thy God!

RUSKIN AND HIS MOTHER

From *Præterita* by John Ruskin

Such being the salutary pleasures of Herne Hill, I have next with deeper gratitude to chronicle what I owed to my mother for the resolutely consistent lessons which so exercised me in the Scriptures as to make every word of them familiar to my ear in habitual music,— yet in that familiarity reverenced, as transcending all thought, and ordaining all conduct.

This she effected, not by her own sayings or personal authority; but simply by compelling me to read the book thoroughly, for myself. As soon as I was able to read with fluency, she began a course of Bible work with me, which never ceased till I went to Oxford. She read alternate verses with me, watching, at first, every intonation of my voice, and correcting the false ones, till she made me understand the verse, if within my reach, rightly, and energetically. . . . In this way she began with the first verse of Genesis, and went through, to the last verse of the Apocalypse; hard names, numbers, Levitical law, and all; and began again at Genesis the next day. If a name was hard, the better the exercise in pronunciation,— if a chapter was tiresome, the better lesson in patience,— if loathsome, the better lesson in faith that there was some use in its being so outspoken. After our chapters, I had to learn a few verses by heart, or repeat, to make sure I had not lost, something of what was already known; and with the chapters thus gradually possessed from the first word to the last, I had to learn the whole body of the fine old Scottish paraphrases, which are good, melodious, and forceful verse; and to which, together with the Bible itself, I owe the first cultivation of my ear sound.

It is strange that of all the pieces of the Bible which my mother thus taught me, that which cost me most to learn, and which was to my child's mind, chiefly repulsive — the 119th Psalm — has now become of all the most precious to me, in its overflowing and glorious passion of love for the Law of God. . . .

But it is only by deliberate effort that I recall the long morning hours of toil, as regular as sunrise,— toil on both sides equal — by which year after year, my mother forced me to learn these paraphrases and chapters, allowing not so much as a syllable to be missed or misplaced; while every sentence was required to be said over and over again till she was satisfied with the accent of it. . . .

And truly, though I have picked up the elements of a little further knowledge — in mathematics, meteorology, and the like, in after life,— and owe not a little to the teaching of many people, this maternal installation of my mind in that property of chapters, I count very confidently the most precious, and, on the whole, the one *essential* part of all my education.

THADDEUS STEVENS

By Phœbe Cary

From the Poetical Works of Alice and Phoebe Cary. Houghton, Mifflin Company.

An eye with the piercing eagle's fire,
　　Not the look of the gentle dove;
Not his the form that men admire,
　　Nor the face that tender women love.

Working first for his daily bread
　　With the humblest toilers of the earth;
Never walking with free, proud tread —
　　Crippled and halting from his birth.

Wearing outside a thorny suit
　　Of sharp, sarcastic, stinging power;
Sweet at the core as sweetest fruit,
　　Or inmost heart of fragrant flower.

Fierce and trenchant, the haughty foe
　　Felt his words like a sword of flame;
But to the humble, poor, and low
　　Soft as a woman's his accents came.

Not his the closest, tenderest friend —
　　No children blessed his lonely way,
But down in his heart until the end
　　The tender dream of his boyhood lay.

His mother's faith he held not fast;
　But he loved her living, mourned her dead,
And kept her memory to the last
　As green as the sod above her bed.

He held as sacred in his home
　Whatever things she wrought or planned,
And never suffered change to come
　To the work of her " industrious hand."

For her who pillowed first his head
　He heaped with a wealth of flowers the grave,
While he chose to sleep in an unmarked bed,
　By his Master's humblest poor — the slave.*

Suppose he swerved from the straightest course —
　That the things he should not do he did —
That he hid from the eyes of mortals close,
　Such sins as you and I have hid?

Or suppose him worse than you; what then?
　Judge not, lest you be judged for sin!
One said who knew the hearts of men:
　Who loveth much shall a pardon win.

The Prince of Glory for sinners bled;
　His soul was bought with a royal price;
And his beautified feet may tread
　To-day with his Lord in Paradise.

　* Thaddeus Stevens, who cared nothing about his own burial-place, ex-
cept that the spot should be one from which the humblest of his fel-
low-creatures were not excluded, left by will one thousand dollars to
beautify and adorn the grave of his mother.

THE MOTHER OF VICTOR HUGO

By Frank T. Marzials

" This century of ours was two years old, the Sparta of the Republic was giving place to the Rome of the Empire, and Bonaparte the First Consul developing into Napoleon the Emperor, . . . when at Besançon . . . there came into the world a child of mingled Breton and Lorraine blood, who was colorless, sightless, voiceless, and so poor a weakling that all despaired of him except his mother. . . . That child, whose name Life appeared to be erasing from its book, and whose short day of existence seemed destined to pass into night with never a morrow — that child am I." Thus in the lines which most Frenchmen know pretty well by heart, has Victor Hugo related the incidents of his birth. To put the matter more prosaically, he was born at Besançon, in the extreme east of France, on February 26, 1802, all declaring that he could not live, the mother fully determined that he *should* live,— and prevailing. Not thus, prematurely, was to close a career destined to be remarkable for its magnificent vitality. " Victor Marie," so was the boy christened and the name proved of happy augury. In the first fight he came off victor over death. Within six weeks he had so far gained strength as to be able to bear removal to Marseilles; and thence, though still very delicate, he was taken about to Corsica and Elba, from station to station, in the wake of a wandering military father. . . .

. . . Nineteen years after the first collection of the " Odes " was published, in June, 1822; and though the book produced much less sensation than had been produced two years before by Lamartine's " Meditations," yet it clearly " numbered good intellects." But that highest pleasure which a first great success can bring was denied to the young poet; his mother had died on the 27th of June, 1821.

Of her a word may fittingly here be said. She was evidently a woman of strong character, trained in habits of independent action by her husband's long absences. Thus she had been led to assume towards her sons, and especially towards the younger two, a position of double parentage. Loving them with a mother's love and entire devotion, she at the same time ruled them with a father's firm hand. Of Victor's capacity she entertained, and with more than abundant cause, a very exalted opinion. " She looked forward," M. Asseline says, " with the greatest confidence to the future of her son, holding that he might, with even greater justice than Fouquet," Louis XIV's overweaning *surintendant*, " adopt as his device the words ' *quo non ascendam?* ' ' to what may I not rise? ' "

That to such a mother Victor should, on his side, have been entirely devoted, was but natural. That her death would leave a terrible blank in his life was clear. It must have made a considerable difference in his circumstances. The father married again. *He* seems to have given his son at this time neither material nor moral support. So the youth of nineteen, left to his own devices, went very sadly on his own way; lived as he could, lived in fact, as he afterwards represented Marius to have lived in "Les Miserables," on almost nothing; — worked very hard; and being out of sorts and quarrelsome, fought a duel with a soldier, who ran him through the arm. "Here am I alone," he wrote a friend two months after his mother's death, "and I have a whole long life to live through, unless " . . .

"Unless!" what does that point to? Suicide, or the possibility of some presence that would make life no longer a solitude? Scarcely the former; for here Love takes a hand in the web of Victor Hugo's story and weaves it with threads of purest gold and silk of daintiest dye; and the fabric so woven is, altogether beautiful.

By permission of the Walter Scott Publishing Company.

MY MOTHER'S PICTURE

By William Cowper

O that those lips had language! Life has passed
With me but roughly since I heard thee last.
Those lips are thine,— thy own sweet smile I see,
The same that oft in childhood solaced me;
Voice only fails, else how distinct they say,
"Grieve not, my child; chase all thy fears away!"
The meek intelligence of those dear eyes
(Blest be the art that can immortalize,—
The art that baffles Time's tyrannic claim
To quench it!) here shines on me still the same.
Faithful remembrancer of one so dear!
O welcome guest though unexpected here!

Who bidst me honor with an artless song,
Affectionate, a mother lost so long.
I will obey,— not willingly alone,
But gladly, as the precept were her own;
And, while that face renews my filial grief,
Fancy shall weave a charm for my relief,—
Shall steep me in Elysian revery,
A momentary dream that thou art she.

 My mother! when I learned that thou wast dead,
Say, wast thou conscious of the tears I shed?
Hovered thy spirit o'er thy sorrowing son,—
Wretch even then, life's journey just begun?
Perhaps thou gavest me, though unfelt, a kiss;
Perhaps a tear, if souls can weep in bliss —
Ah! that maternal smile! it answers — Yes.
I heard the bell tolled on the burial day;
I saw the hearse that bore thee slow away;
And, turning from my nursery window, drew
A long, long sigh, and wept a last adieu!

 But was it such? — It was.— Where thou art gone
Adieus and farewells are a sound unknown.
May I but meet thee on that peaceful shore,
The parting word shall pass my lips no more.
Thy maidens, grieved at my concern,
Oft gave me promise of thy quick return;
What ardently I wished I long believed,
And, disappointed still, was still deceived,—
By expectation every day beguiled,
Dupe of to-morrow even from a child.
Thus many a sad to-morrow came and went,
Till, all my stock of infant sorrows spent,

I learned at last submission to my lot;
But, though I less deplored thee, ne'er forgot.

Where once we dwelt our name is heard no more;
Children not thine have trod my nursery floor;
And where the gardener Robin, day by day,
Drew me to school along the public way,—
Delighted with my bawble coach, and wrapped
In scarlet mantle warm and velvet capped—
'Tis now become a history little known
That once we called the pastoral house our own.
Short-lived possession! but the record fair,
That memory keeps of all thy kindness there,
Still outlives many a storm that has effaced
A thousand other themes, less deeply traced:
Thy nightly visits to my chamber made,
That thou mightst know me safe and warmly laid;
Thy morning bounties ere I left my home,—
The biscuit, or confectionery plum;
The fragrant waters on my cheeks bestowed
By thy own hand, till fresh they shone and glowed,—
All this, and, more endearing still than all,
Thy constant flow of love that knew no fall,—
Ne'er roughened by those cataracts and breaks
That humor interposed too often makes;
All this still legible in memory's page,
And still to be so till my latest age,
Adds joy to duty, makes me glad to pay
Such honors to thee as my numbers may,—
Perhaps a frail memorial, but sincere,—
Not scorned in heaven, though little noticed here.

Could Time, his flight reversed, restore the hours

When playing with thy vesture's tissued flowers,—
The violet, the pink, the jassamine,—
I pricked them into paper with a pin,
(And thou wast happier than myself the while —
Wouldst softly speak, and stroke my head and smile,)
Could those few pleasant days again appear,
Might one wish bring them, would I wish them here?
I would not trust my heart,— the dear delight
Seems so to be desired, perhaps I might —
But no — what here we call our life is such,
So little to be loved, and thou so much,
That I should ill requite thee to constrain
Thy unbound spirit into bonds again.
 Thou — as a gallant bark, from Albion's coast,
(The storms all weathered and the ocean crossed,)
Shoots into port at some well-havened isle,
Where spices breathe and brighter seasons smile:
There sits quiescent on the floods, that show
Her beauteous form reflected clear below,
While airs impregnated with incense play
Around her, fanning light her streamers gay,—
So thou, with sails how swift! hast reached the shore
"Where tempests never beat nor billows roar,"
And thy loved consort on the dangerous tide
Of life long since has anchored by thy side.
But me, scarce hoping to attain that rest,
Always from port withheld, always distressed,—
Me howling blasts drive devious, tempest-tossed,
Sails ripped, seams opening wide, and compass lost;
And day by day some current's thwarting force
Sets me more distant from a prosperous course.

Yet O, the thought that thou art safe, and he! —
That thought is joy, arrive what may to me.
My boast is not that I deduce my birth
From loins enthroned, and rulers of the earth;
But higher far my proud pretensions rise,—
The son of parents passed into the skies.
And now, farewell! — Time, unrevoked, has run
His wonted course; yet what I wished is done.
By contemplation's help, not sought in vain,
I seem to have lived my childhood o'er again,—
To have renewed the joys that once were mine,
Without the sin of violating thine;
And, while the wings of fancy still are free,
And I can view this mimic show of thee,
Time has but half succeeded in his theft,—
Thyself removed, they power to soothe me left.

THE MOTHER OF FRANCES WILLARD

By Anna Adams Gordon

"There are not many men, and as yet but few
women, of whom when you think or speak it occurs
to you that they are great," said Miss Willard.

"What is the line that could mark such a sphere?
To my mind it must include this trinity — greatness
of thought, of heart, of will. There have been men
and women concerning whose greatness of intellect
none disputed, but they were poverty-stricken in the
region of the affections, or they were Lilliputians in
the realm of the will. There have been mighty hearts,

beating strong and full as a ship's engine, but they were mated to a 'straightened forehead.' There have been Napoleonic wills, but unbalanced by strong power of thought and sentiment — they were like a cyclone or a wandering star. It takes force centrifugal and force centripetal to balance a character to the ellipse of a true orbit.

"My mother, my Saint Courageous, was great in the sense of this majestic symmetry. The classic writer who said, 'I am human, and whatever touches humanity touches me,' could not have been more worthy to utter the words than was this Methodist cosmopolite who spoke them to me within a few days of her ascent to heaven. She had no pettiness. It was the habit of her mind to study subjects from the point of harmony. She did not say, 'Wherein does this Baptist or this Presbyterian differ from the creed in which I have been reared?' But it was as natural to her as it is to the rose to give forth fragrance to say to herself and others: 'Wherein does this Presbyterian or Baptist harmonize with the views that are dear to me?' Then she dwelt upon that harmony and through it brought those about her into oneness of sympathy with herself. She was occupied with great themes. I never heard a word of gossip from her lips. She had no time for it. Her life illustrated the poet's line:

There is no finer flower on this green earth than courage.

"My mother had courage of intellect and heart, and physical courage as well, beyond any other woman I have known. 'We are saved by hope,' was the motto of her life. ' This is our part and all the part we have,' she used to say. ' The existence and love of God are the pulse of our being, whether we live or die.'

" Some characters have a great and varied landscape, and a light like that of Raphael's pictures; others show forth some strong, single feature in a light like that of Rembrandt; some have headlands and capes, bays and skies, meadows and prairies and seas. The more scenery there is in a character, the greater it is — the more it ranges from the amusing to the sublime. My mother's nature had in it perspective, atmosphere, landscape of earth and sky.

" She was not given to introspection, which is so often the worm in the bud of genius. ' They are not great who counsel with their fears.' Applied Christianity was the track along which the energy of her nature was driven by the Divine Spirit.

" The fortunes of the great white-ribbon cause gave her a pedestal to stand upon. She had been, in her beautiful home, a mother so beloved that she drew all her household toward her as the sun does the planets round about him, but she became a mother to our whole army. She came to the kingdom for a sorrowful time, when the homes were shadowed over all the land and her motherly nature found a circle as wide as the shadow cast upon the republic by the nation's dark eclipse. Perhaps, until then, she had not been a radical so pronounced as she became in these later battle years, but what she saw and learned and suffered, out in the cross-currents of society and the

great world, made her as strong a believer in the
emancipation of woman as any person whom I have
ever met. She had no harsh word for anybody; no
criticism on the past. She recognized the present sit-
uation as the inevitable outcome of the age of force,
but her great soul was suffused to its last fiber with
the enthusiasm for woman. She believed in her sex;
she had pride in it; she regarded its capacities of mental
and moral improvement as illimitable, but at the same
time she was a devoted friend to men. How could
she be otherwise with a husband true and loyal and
with a loving and genial son? All her ideas on the
woman question were but a commentary upon her de-
votion to that larger human question which is the
great circle of which the woman question is but an
arc."

The following reference to Madam Willard's charm-
ing methods of child culture is given by her daughter:

"She never expected us to be bad children. I
never heard her refer to total depravity as our in-
evitable heritage; she always said when we were
cross, 'Where is my bright little girl that is so pleas-
ant to have about? Somebody must have taken her
away and left this little creature here who has a scowl
upon her face.' She always expected us to do well.
She used to say that a little child is a figure of pathos.
Without volition of its own, it finds itself in a most
difficult scene; it looks around on every side for help,
and we who are grown way-wise should make it feel
at all times tenderly welcome, and nourish it in the

fruitful atmosphere of love, trust, and approbation.

"With such a mother, my home life was full of inspiration; she encouraged every out-branching thought and purpose. When I wished to play out-of-doors with my brother, and do the things he did, she never said, 'Oh, that is not for girls!' but encouraged him to let me be his little comrade; by which means he became the most considerate, chivalric boy I ever knew, for his mother taught him that nothing could be more for her happiness and his than that he should be good to 'little sister.' By this means I spent a great deal of time in the open air, and learned the pleasant sports by which boys store up vigor for the years to come.

"To my mind the jewel of her character and method with her children was that she knew how without effort to keep an open way always between her inmost heart and theirs; they wanted no other comforter; everybody seemed less desirable than mother. If something very pleasant happened to us when we were out playing with other children, or spending an afternoon at a neighbor's, we would scamper home as fast as our little feet would carry us, because we did not feel as if we had gained the full happiness from anything that came to us until mother knew it."

Sir Walter Scott tells a story of a brave young knight in whose soul burned the Crusader's passion to rescue from the infidels' defiling hands the tomb of his hero-Christ. Girding on the shield and buckler and sword, he knelt before the woman who through the years had given her life to him in lavishment of mother-love and claimed her mother-blessing on his eager heart's desire. With never a falter of voice or a sob to betray her anguish of grief and fear, with never a tremble in the hand that touched his bright young head, with only courage in tender tone and touch, she sent him forth, inspired by her blessing under the banner of her love. In his garments she hid her jewels against his hour of need, and with the promise that she would stay at home and guard for him his castle and his lands, she bade him depart, remembering that his glory was to redress human wrongs, to keep a spotless sword and soul. When many years had come and gone and the youth returned crowned with victories won on many a field where he had vanquished wrong, he found his castle and his lands better cared for than when he left, his people taught to reverence his name and to love him for his knightly deeds.

This beautiful picture of the Scottish novelist's but faintly sets forth the work of that noble mother, " Saint Courageous," who, when the daughter went forth the " Knight of a New Chivalry," kept the fires of love burning brightly upon her hearth, kept the light in the window for the brave daughter who went forth on her crusade pilgrimages, not to save an empty tomb, but to rescue the living Christ in human hearts from the enemies that defile the temple of God.

To the music of the Traveler's Psalm (cxxi), accompanied by the strong, tender voice of commending prayer, Mother Willard sent forth her apostle of sweetness and purity and light, even as of old that English mother commended her young knight to the guidance of Him who had promised victory to all who war against iniquity and sin. And to that heart and home the gentle conqueror hastened back less like a victor to claim her own than like a bird to its sheltering nest. Here one month at least of every year was given to her mother, that the springs of love and hope and inspiration might be refilled. Sitting by the fire with clasped hands, the mother would give to her daughter reminiscences of her early life, telling her of the beautiful Christian traits of her father and mother; recalling to mind the older home in Vermont; describing the noble hills upon which her windows looked; recounting the way she spent her days, the morning hours given to books and study, the afternoons to weaving, spinning, and household cares, the evenings spent again about the fireside, until when nine o'clock struck, the entire household assembled while her father read from the dear old Bible and, by the force of fervent prayer, drew them all within the circle of divine protection and love.

Often the household saint would break forth into words of gratitude for the long life that had been so rich in opportunity, so blessed with friendships and affection. Often she rejoiced in the good gift of the uninterrupted strength that enabled her to fill all the years with toil.

" I must keep well for the sake of my daughter and the work God has given her to do," would say this sympathetic mother, who in her seventieth year led the Woman's Christian Temperance Union of her own town. If the daughter encircled the world with the white ribbon of love and sympathy, the threads of that shining strand were surely spun in the warp and woof of her mother's loving care.

Recalling her first visit to Rest Cottage, Lady Henry Somerset, whom Madam Willard fondly called her "English daughter," writes:

"When I came to your shores a stranger a year ago the name of Frances Willard was as familiar to me as it is to women all over the world who are in any way associated with the works of philanthropy or the upbuilding of the home. I had read her life and had some knowledge of her work, and with that work of course her mother's name was closely associated. But only when I crossed the threshold of Rest Cottage could I realize what a factor that mother had been in her great career. I have mingled with those who are called noble because of hereditary descent; I have talked with empresses and queens, with princesses and princes, but when I took the hand of Madam Willard and she welcomed me to her heart and home, I knew instantly and instinctively that here was one of the world's great women. A lady of such fine, delicate instinct, with a mind so cultivated and purified by continued aspiration toward the good and true; with a face serene and full of all that inherent worth which came to her through her spotless ancestry and her own natural purity and refinement, I at once classed with all the greatest and noblest that I had ever met. I need not dwell here upon the way in which that home circle impressed me, but as I turn the pages of my Bible, I find a note entered there which I wrote the first night I came beneath that roof: 'October 28, 1891 — A day to be remembered in thanksgiving. Rest Cottage, Evanston.' "

It was the going from life of such a mother that made earth empty and the heart of the daughter forever bereaved. Ever after, her spirit drooped; a part of Miss Willard's deeper spiritual self reached out toward that universe to which from the moment of her mother's departure she felt she too belonged. In her journal we find the ever-recurring eloquent question, "Where is my mother?" A question that was to persistently reiterate itself until, like a tired child, she had been restored to her mother's arms. Not otherwise than Monica and Saint Augustine did these two, "Saint Courageous" and her daughter Frances, sit in the open window and gaze into the open sky into which the mother was soon to take her flight; they saw the heavens open and those who once had dwelt within their home, standing by the throne of God. If in the supreme hour of entrance upon the life with God, the mother ascending sent benediction down upon her daughter and upon all the world, the daughter, gazing into the open sky, cried out, "I give thee joy, my mother! All hail, but not farewell. Our faces are set the same way, blessed mother. I shall follow after — it will not be long."

In the sunset years of her mother's life Miss Willard had centralized her work in the beloved home, now adorned by countless kindnesses of comrades and friends. Picturing the busy hours in the cozy "den" when, shut in with that serene and benignant being "Saint Courageous," Miss Willard was lifted above her former toilsome life, we are reminded of her journal note, written when, as a young teacher in Kankakee, she mused on the home faces of her " Four ":

" I thank God for my mother as for no other gift of His bestowing. My nature is so woven into hers that I almost think it would be death for me to have the bond severed and one so much myself gone over the river. She does not know, they do not any of them, the ' Four,' how much my mother is to me, for, as I verily believe, I cling to her more than ever did any other of her children. Perhaps because I am to need her more."

Surely, she who could bear and train such a daughter was worthy to be what she always remained — her inspiration and her ideal.

At the close of the Buffalo convention of the World's Christian Temperance Union, in 1897, Miss Willard went to Churchville, N. Y., her birthplace, for a Sunday with beloved relatives. The morning was spent with the only surviving relative of her mother's generation, " Aunt Sarah," and in the afternoon she met the white-ribboners in the Methodist church. After the service, two by two they walked to the house where Miss Willard was born. Seeking out the very room into which the little stranger came, standing closely about their leader they heard her talk of motherhood and of the great home to which she was looking, now that her mother's ear would never again hear her returning footsteps. It was in that room the mother-love had hung over the cradle of the child Frances, as the star hung over the babe in the manger of Bethlehem.

It was her birth that called forth these words of Mrs. Willard in the last year of her earthly life:

" Motherhood is life's richest and most delicious romance. And sitting now in the sunshine calm and sweet, with all my precious ones on the other side save only the daughter who so faithfully cherishes me here, I thank God that he ever said to me ' Bring up this child for me in the love of humanity and the expectation of immortal life.' My life could not have held more joy, if some white-robed messenger of the skies had come to me and said, ' I will send a spiritual being into your arms and home. It is a momentous charge, potent for good or evil, but I will help you. Do not fear. Therefore, mother, step softly. Joy shall be the accepted creed of this young immortal in all the coming years. This child shall herald your example and counsels when you are resting from your labors.' "

Miss Willard lived six years after her mother's death. These years were spent in America, and in England with her friend Lady Henry Somerset. The friendship of these two meant so much to both women personally as well as to the cause they represented and to womanhood in the mother country and the home land. Miss Willard as the Founder and President of The World's Woman's Christian Temperance Union was greeted with great ovations. At a meeting at Exeter Hall at which at least five thousand people were present Lady Henry in an eloquent address of welcome presented the woman and the work they had gathered to honor. Among her words are these:

" Sacrifice is the foundation of all real success, and

it was a crucial moment in Miss Willard's life when she deliberately relinquished the brilliant position of dean of the first woman's college connected with a university in America, to go out penniless, alone, and and unheralded, because her spirit had caught the rhythm of the women's footsteps as they bridged the distance between the home and the saloon in the Pentecostal days of the temperance crusade. She has relinquished that which women hold the dearest — the sacred, sheltered life of home. For her no children wait around the Christmas hearth, but she has lost that life only to find it again ten thousand fold. She has understood the mystery of the wider circle of love and loyalty, and the world is her home as truly as it was John Wesley's 'parish.' She has understood the divine motherhood that claims the orphaned hearts of humanity for her heritage, and a chorus of children's voices around the world hail her as mother, for organized mother-love is the best definition of the Woman's Christian Temperance Union."

Frances Willard died as triumphant as she had lived. From the first of her illness she felt she might not recover, but her physician was hopeful and assured her that her earthly work was not done. She was resting after talking on her last afternoon on earth and seemed to be unconscious when a friend came into the room. As her hand was quietly touched she looked up, and recognizing the kind face of her comrade, said with a faint smile, " I've crept in with mother and it is the same beautiful world and the same people; remember that — *it's just the same.*" . . .

On Sunday afternoon, April tenth, 1898, amid the
Easter sunshine, a hushed and reverent company gath-
ered at the Willard lot in Rosehill cemetery. The
grave of Miss Willard's mother was opened, the sides
lined with evergreens, the mound of earth also hidden
by green boughs. As the sacred ashes were literally
committed to the precious dust beneath them, they
mingled with white roses, above which were placed
sprays of evergreen, sent from the birthplaces of Miss
Willard's parents, of her brother and sister, and of
herself, and from Forest Home and Rest Cottage; then
all was made radiant with bright blossoms, emblems of
the glorious springtime. A moss-covered box, fra-
grant with lilies of the valley and pansies, and which
had held a precious inner box of purest white, was
placed over the mother's heart. Surrounding the
whole, in beauty and fragrance, were the floral tributes
of friends, and thus Frances Willard, that great woman
who had never lost her childhood, at last " crept in with
mother."

*From " The Life of Frances E. Willard," by Anna A. Gordon, pub-
lished by National Woman's Christian Temperance Union, Evanston, Ill.*

THE MOTHER OF EUGENE FIELD

By IDA COMSTOCK BELOW

Eugene Field's mother (Frances Reed) was a hand-
some woman, possessed of great strength of character,
which was accompanied by rare sweetness and gentle-
ness. Although only a boy of six when he lost his
mother, he said: " I have carried the remembrance of
her gentle voice and soothing touch all through my

life." One can easily imagine the sorrow of such a
child for the loss of such a mother. It was only in
later years, however, that he gave expression to his
heart-longing for her, in the beautiful lines:

TO MY MOTHER

How fair you are, my mother!
  Ah, though 't is many a year
  Since you were here,
Still do I see your beauteous face,
  And with the glow
Of your dark eyes cometh a grace
  Of long ago.

So gentle, too, my mother!
  Just as of old, upon my brow,
  Like benedictions now,
Falleth your hand's touch;
  And still, as then,
A voice that glads me overmuch
  Cometh again,
My fair and gentle mother!

How you have loved me, mother,
  I have not power to tell,
  Knowing full well
That even in the rest above
  It is your will
To watch and guard me with your love,
  Loving me still.

And as of old, my mother,
   I am content to be a child,
   By mother's love beguiled
From all these other charms;
   So to the last
Within thy dear protecting arms
   Hold thou me fast,
My guardian angel, mother!

THE MOTHER OF HARRIET B. STOWE *

From Autobiography and Correspondence of Lyman Beecher

In one of the Mayflower sketches, in the character of Aunt Mary, and later, in a letter contributed to the "Autobiography of Lyman Beecher," Mrs. Stowe herself describes her mother:

"My dear Brother,— I was between three and four years of age when our mother died, and my own personal recollections of her are therefore but few. But the deep interest and veneration that she inspired in all who knew her was such that, during my childhood, I was constantly hearing her spoken of, and, from one friend or another, some incident or anecdote of her life was constantly being impressed on me.

"Mother was one of those strong, restful, yet widely sympathetic natures, in whom all around seemed to find comfort and repose. She was of a temperament peculiarly restful and peace-giving. Her union of spirit with God, unruffled and unbroken even from early childhood, seemed to impart to her an equilibrium and healthful placidity that no earthly reverses ever disturbed. The communion between her and my father was a peculiar one. It was an intimacy throughout the whole range of their being. There was no human mind in whose decisions he had greater confidence. Both intellectually and morally he regarded her as the better and stronger portion of himself, and I remember hearing him say that, after her death, his first sensation was a sort of terror, like that of a child suddenly shut out alone in the dark.

" Her death occurred at a time when the New England ministry were in a peculiar crisis of political and moral trial, and the need of such a stay and support in his household was more than ever felt.

" He told me that at this time he was so oppressed by the constant turning toward her of thoughts and feelings which he had constantly been in the habit of speaking to her, that, merely to relieve himself, he once sat down and wrote to her a letter, in which he poured out all his soul. . . .

" In my own early childhood only two incidents of my mother twinkle like rays through the darkness. One was of our running and dancing out before her from the nursery to the sitting room one Sabbath morning, and her pleasant voice saying after us, ' Remember the Sabbath day to keep it holy.'

" Another remembrance is this : Mother was an enthusiastic horticulturist in all the small ways that limited means allowed. Her brother John, in New

York, had just sent her a small parcel of fine tulip-bulbs. I remember rummaging these out of an obscure corner of the nursery one day when she was gone out, and being strongly seized with the idea that they were good to eat, and using all the little English I then possessed to persuade my brothers that these were onions such as grown people ate, and would be very nice for us. So we fell to and devoured the whole; and I recollect being somewhat disappointed in the odd, sweetish taste, and thinking that onions were not as nice as I had supposed. Then mother's serene face appeared at the nursery door, and we all ran toward her, and with one voice began to tell our discovery and achievement. We had found this bag of onions, and had eaten them all up.

"Also I remember that there was not even a momentary expression of impatience, but that she sat down and said, 'My dear children, what you have done makes mamma very sorry; those were not onion-roots, but roots of beautiful flowers; and if you had let them alone, mamma would have had next summer in her garden great beautiful red and yellow flowers such as you never saw!' I remember how drooping and dispirited we all grew at this picture, and how sadly we regarded the empty bag.

"Then I have a recollection of her reading to the children one evening aloud Miss Edgeworth's 'Frank' which had just come out, I believe, and was exciting a good deal of attention among the educational circles at Litchfield. After that I remember a time when every one said she was sick, when, if I went into the street, every one asked me how my mother was; when I saw the shelves of the closets crowded with delicacies which had been sent in for her, and how I used to be permitted to go once a day into her room, where she sat bolstered up in bed, taking her gruel. I have a vision of a very fair face, with a bright red spot on each cheek, and a quiet smile as she offered me a spoonful of her gruel; of our dreaming one night, we little ones, that mamma had got well, and waking in loud transports of joy, and being hushed down by some one coming into the room. Our dream was indeed a true one. She was forever well; but they told us she was dead, and took us to see what seemed so cold, and so unlike anything we had ever seen or known of her.

"Then came the funeral. Henry was too little to go. I remember his golden curls and little black frock, as he frolicked like a kitten in the sun in ignorant joy.

"I remember the mourning dresses, the tears of the older children, the walking to the burial-ground, and somebody's speaking at the grave, and the audible sobbing of the family; and then all was closed, and we little ones, to whom it was so confused, asked the question where she was gone, and would she never come back?

"They told us at one time that she had been laid in the ground, at another that she had gone to heaven; whereupon Henry, putting the two things together, resolved to dig through the ground and go to heaven to find her; for, being discovered under sister Catharine's window one morning digging with great zeal and earnestness, she called to him to know what he was doing, and, lifting his curly head with great simplicity, he answered, ' Why, I'm going to heaven to find Mamma.'

" Although mother's bodily presence disappeared from our circle, I think that her memory and example had more influence in molding her family, in deterring from evil and exciting to good, than the living presence of many mothers. It was a memory that met us everywhere, for every person in town, from the highest to the lowest, seemed to have been so impressed by her character and life that they constantly reflected some portion of it back on us.

" Even our portly old black washerwoman, Candace, who came once a week to help off the great family wash, would draw us aside, and, with tears in her eyes, tell us of the saintly virtues of our mother.

" The traditions that I heard from my aunts and uncles were such as these : ' Your mother never spoke an angry word in her life. Your mother never told a lie.' And in Nutplains and Guilford, where her early days were passed, I used to find myself treated with a tenderness almost amounting to veneration by those who had known her.

" I recollect, too, that at first the house was full of little works of ingenuity, and taste, and skill, which had been wrought by her hand ; exquisite needle-work, which has almost passed out of memory in our day. . . .

" One thing in her personal appearance every one

spoke of, that she never spoke in company or before strangers without blushing. She was of such great natural sensitiveness and even timidity that, in some respects she could never conform to the standard of what was expected of a pastor's wife. In the weekly female prayer-meetings she could never lead the devotions. Yet it was not known that any body ever expressed criticism or censure on this account. It somehow seemed to be felt that her silent presence had more power than the audible exercises of another. Such impression has been given me by those who have spoken of this peculiarity.

" There was one passage of Scripture always associated with her in our minds in childhood; it was this: ' Ye are come unto Mount Zion the city of the living God, to the heavenly Jerusalem, and to an innumerable company of angels; to the general assembly and Church of the first-born, and to the spirits of just men made perfect.' We all knew that this was what our father repeated to her when she was dying, and we often repeated it to each other. It was to that we felt we *must* attain, though we scarcely knew how. In every scene of family joy or sorrow, or when father wished to make an appeal to our hearts which he knew we could not resist, he spoke of mother.

" I remember still the solemn impression produced on my mind when I was only eight years old. I had been violently seized with malignant scarlet fever, and lain all day insensible, and father was in an agony of apprehension for my life. I remember waking up just as the beams of the setting sun were shining into the window, and hearing his voice in prayer by my bedside, and of his speaking of 'her blessed mother who is now a saint in heaven,' and wondering in my heart what that solemn appeal might mean.

"I think it will be the testimony of all her sons that her image stood between them and the temptations of youth as a sacred shield; that the hope of meeting her in heaven has sometimes been the last strand which did not part in hours of fierce temptation; and that the remembrance of her holy life and death was a solemn witness of the truth of religion, which repelled every assault of scepticism, and drew back the soul from every wandering, to the faith in which she lived and died.

"The passage in 'Uncle Tom,' where St. Clare describes his mother's influence, is a simple reproduction of this mother's influence as it has always been in the family.

"The following lines, written by her eldest daughter, Catharine, then a girl of sixteen, were a tribute offered to her memory. We knew them by heart in our childhood, and often repeated them with tears:

"The busy hum of day is o'er,
　　The scene is sweet and still,
And modest eve, with blushes warm,
　　Walks o'er the western hill.

.　　.　　.　　.　　.　　.　　.　　.

"The great, the good, the rich, the wise,
　　Lie shrouded here in gloom;

And here with aching heart I view
   My own dear mother's tomb.

" Oh, as upon her peaceful grave
   I fix my weeping eyes,
How many fond remembrances
   In quick succession rise.

" Far through the vista of past years
   As memory can extend,
She walked, my counselor and guide,
   My guardian and friend.

" From works of science and of taste,
   How richly stored her mind;
And yet how mild in all her ways,
   How gentle meek and kind.

" Religion's bless'd and heavenly light
   Illumined all her road;
Before her house she led the way
   To virtue and to God.

" Like some fair orb she bless'd my way
   With mild and heavenly light,
Till, called from hence, the opening heav'n
   Received her from my sight.

.   .   .   .

" Now left in dark and dubious night,
   I mourn her guidance o'er,

And sorrow that my longing eyes
  Shall see her face no more.

.   .   .   .

" Father in heaven, my mother's God,
  Oh grant before thy seat,
Among the blessed sons of light,
  Parent and child may meet.

.   .   .   .

" There may I see her smiling face,
  And hear her gentle voice;
And, gladdened by thy gracious smile,
  Through endless years rejoice."

Reprinted by permission of Harper and Brothers.

CHRIST THE MENDICANT

By John B. Tabb

A Stranger, to His own
He came; and one alone,
Who knew not sin,
His lowliness believed,
And in her soul conceived
To let Him in.

He naked was, and she
Of her humanity
A garment wove:
He hungered; and she gave,
What most His heart did crave,
A Mother's love.

THE MOTHER OF WASHINGTON

By William M. Thayer

From *Turning Points in Successful Careers*

George Washington's mother was a woman of strong character, of whom George Washington Parke Custis wrote:

" The mother held in reserve an authority which never departed from her, not even when her son had become the most illustrious of men.   It seemed to say, ' I am your mother, the being who gave you life, the guide who directed your steps when they needed the guidance of age and wisdom, the parental affection which claimed your love, the parental authority which commanded your obedience; whatever may be your success, whatever your renown, next to your God, you owe them most to me.'   Nor did the chief dissent from these truths; but to the last moments of the life of his venerable parent, he yielded to her will the most dutiful and implicit obedience, and felt for her person and character the most holy reverence and attachment."

Historians and poets, statesmen and orators, have ever accorded to the mother of Washington a signal influence in determining his character and career. So universal is this sentiment, that the American people consider the noblest tribute to her memory is the inscription upon her monument, " MARY, THE MOTHER OF WASHINGTON."

. . . His school days closed a month before his sixteenth birthday.   His vacations, and such other times as he could command, were spent with his brother Lawrence at his home. Lawrence was a military officer, and his residence was the temporary home of other military men. George enjoyed their company, and became somewhat fascinated with military life, for which Lawrence thought he was especially adapted. For this reason he proposed that George should become a midshipman on a British man-of-war. The proposition fired the soul of our young hero, and he besought his brother to obtain the consent of his mother. After much conversation, explanation, and pleading, Lawrence obtained the consent of his mother; and, soon after, a British man-of-war moved up the Potomac, and cast anchor in full sight of Mount Vernon. On board this vessel a midshipman's warrant was obtained for George, who was more elated over this bit of fortune than over any previous experience of his life. What had been a sort of dream to him had suddenly become reality. His preparation for departure was soon made. His trunk was packed and carried on board the ship that would bear him away from his native land. He was arrayed in the gay uniform of a midshipman, and nothing remained but to bid his mother and other relatives farewell.

But when he stood before his mother in his naval costume, so tall and robust in figure, so handsome and graceful, so noble in appearance, the thought that she might never behold him again completely overcame her usual firmness and self-control, and she burst into tears. " I cannot let you go ! " she exclaimed : " it will break my heart, George." The son was taken by surprise, and well-nigh unmanned at the sight of his mother in tears. "But how can I refuse to go now that I have enlisted, and my trunk is on board?" he said. "Order your trunk ashore, and return your uniform, my son, if you do not wish to crush your mother's heart," nervously and feelingly answered Mrs. Washington, "I cannot bear the thought."

It was a trying ordeal for George; a sudden and sharp turn to make in his life, if he yielded to her request. But fortunately for him and the American republic, he made it in the manliness of his soul. "Mother, I can never go and cause you so much grief. I will stay at home," he answered. Then it was that "Washington the Father of his Country," was assured, and the Declaration of American Independence promised! We are not competent to say exactly what might have been the result to this country had George persisted to be a midshipman in the service of the king; but we are certainly justified in saying there would have been no Brandywine and Valley Forge, no Monmouth and Yorktown. The mother's tears blasted the hopes of the delighted midshipman, but made it possible for freedom to rear its temple on these shores.

THE MOTHER OF THE WESLEYS

By Kirke White

It is generally known that Providence blessed Mrs. Wesley and her husband with nineteen children. It is difficult to ascertain how many of this large number were living at one time. Only seven daughters and three sons grew up to maturity. But John Wesley speaks with profound admiration of the serenity with which his Mother wrote letters, attended to business, and held conversations while surrounded by *thirteen* children. More than ten, therefore, must have survived the period of infancy.

These repeated bereavements were borne with becoming resignation to the Divine will; but they, nevertheless, deeply wrung the Mother's heart. One sentence, penned many years after they had taken place, discloses the feeling with which she remembers her losses:—" I have buried many! — but here I must pause!"

Mrs. Wesley's care for those who died in childhood was soon over but the ten survivors claimed her untiring attention and industry for many years. Her marvelous ability and success in their education and training, have won for her a proud, if not preëminent position among the many illustrious mothers of the wise and good. On all hands, her sons and daughters are acknowledged to form one of the most remarkable family groups in the history of English households; and their eminence is largely attributed to their early domestic training. It therefore becomes a deeply interesting inquiry,— what were the means by which their various powers were so admirably developed, and their character so well and firmly built up?

Using the word education in its widest sense, it is obvious that the bodily appetites and wants of the

child first demand the parent's careful attention.   Mrs.
Wesley was so well persuaded of this that no sooner
were her children born into the world, than their in-
fant life was regulated by method.   Even their sleep
was meted out in strict accordance with rule.   The ap-
pointed time for their slumbers — three hours in the
morning and three in the afternoon,— was gradually
shortened, until they required none at all during the
day-time.   Punctual to the moment were they laid in
the cradle, and rocked to sleep.   The gentle motion
was continued until the allotted time, and then, asleep
or awake, they were taken up.   At seven o'clock, im-
mediately after supper they were prepared for bed;
and at eight they were left in their several rooms
awake; " for there was no such thing allowed in the
house as sitting by a child until it went asleep."

As soon " as they were grown pretty strong," they
were confined to three meals a day.   Eating between
the appointed hours was never allowed " except in case
of sickness, which seldom happened."   At breakfast
they always had " spoon meat "; and sometimes the
same at supper, as soon as family prayers were over.
At these meals they were never allowed to " eat of
more than one thing, and of that sparingly enough."
Dinner was a more ample repast.   " Their little table
and chairs," says Mrs. Wesley, " were set by ours,
where they could be overlooked.   As soon as they
could handle a knife and fork," they were promoted
to a seat at the regular family table.   In all cases it
was an imperative law, that they should eat and drink
what was set before them.

. . . Mrs. Wesley's rule over her children became one of absolute authority, blended with the strongest maternal love. She moved among them, not as a mere school-mistress, punctilious only about the observance of routine and rule; but as a mother, allowed of God to be put in trust for their education, and yearning for the welfare of their souls. Duty was never made hateful by being assigned as a punishment. All her commands were pleasant, her rebukes were always well-timed; proportioned as nearly as possible to the offense; never adminstered in anger, but as the remonstrances of a tender mother. . . .

The communication of intellectual instruction must necessarily enter largely into every system of education. Mrs. Wesley never attempted to teach her children even the letters of the alphabet, until they had completed their fifth year. But no sooner was the appointed birthday with its simple festivities fairly over, than learning began in earnest. The day before the new pupil took his formal place in the school-room " the house was set in order, every one's work appointed, and a charge given that no one should come into the room from nine till twelve, or from two till five." The allotted task for those six hours was for the new scholar to acquire a perfect mastery of the alphabet and in every case, save two, the evening of the day saw Mrs. Wesley's children in full possession of the elements of future learning.

The next step instead of going over a page of uninteresting and unmeaning syllables, which communicate no thoughts to the mind, the pupil was taken at

once to the sublime announcement;—" In the beginning
God created the heaven and the earth." This he was
taught to spell, syllable by syllable, and word by word;
" then to read it over and over, until he could read it
off-hand without hesitation." He then proceeded with
the next verse in the chapter in the same way; and was
never allowed to leave off until perfect in the ap-
pointed lesson. In these initiatory stages there was
the most resolute perseverance until the child gained
a thorough mastery of his task. " I wonder at your
patience," said her husband on one occasion: " You
have told that child twenty times the same thing."
" Had I satisfied myself by mentioning the matter only
nineteen times," replied Mrs. Wesley, " I should have
lost all my labor. You see it was the twentieth time
that crowned the whole." Under such teaching, all
preliminary difficulties vanished away in a few days,
and reading became easy, instructive, and pleasant.

In some of these details Mrs. Wesley was probably
influenced by a singular fact in connection with her
eldest child. His hearing was acute and perfect; his
intellect apparently keen and active: but there was no
power of speech. He never uttered an intelligible word
until he was nearly five years old; and his parents
began to fear that he was hopelessly dumb. Having
been missed longer than usual on one occasion, his
mother sought him in different parts of the house,
but without success. Becoming alarmed, she called him
loudly by name, and to her joyful surprise, he answered
from under the table, in a clear distinct voice, " Here
I am, Mother!" Suddenly, and without any assign-

able reason for effort, he had gained the use of speech. This early infirmity in the case of her first-born prevented Mrs. Wesley beginning to teach him, had she been so disposed, before he was five years old. He learned with great rapidity, " and had such a prodigious memory," writes his Mother, " that I cannot remember to have told him the same word twice. What was still stranger, any word he had learned in his lesson, he knew whenever he saw it, either in his Bible or any other book: by which means he learned very soon to read an English author well." This was her first attempt at teaching; and its great and cheering success probably fixed her future plans of action, from which she never deviated, except in the case of her youngest child. With her she was persuaded to commence teaching before the five years had expired, " and she was more years learning than any of the rest had been months."

The school always opened and closed with singing a solemn psalm, and was a scene of perfect order, nothing being permitted to interrupt the regular course of study. " If visitors, business, or accident be allowed to interfere with reading, working, or singing psalms at the appointed times, you will find such impediments multiplied upon you, till at last all order and devotion will be lost." Everything moved according to rule. " Every one was kept close to their business for the six hours." There was no loud talking or playing. " Rising out of their places, or going out of the room was not permitted, unless for good cause; and running into the yard, garden, or street, without leave, was always esteemed a capital offense." With such teaching and discipline, no wonder that the progress of the learners was uniformly rapid and satisfactory. " And it is almost incredible," adds Mrs. Wesley, " what a child may be taught in a quarter of a year, by a vigorous application, if it have but a tolerable capacity and good health."

If, therefore, it be open to doubt whether there be any definite rule for the time of commencing, or the best mode of communicating intellectual instruction in all cases, there can be no question that Mrs. Wesley's system, as carried out in her own family, was amply justified by its satisfactory results.

THE MOTHER OF LAMARTINE *

From *Memoirs of My Youth*

My education was wholly centered in the glance more or less serene and the smile, more or less open of my mother. The reins of my heart were in her hand. She asked nothing from me but to be truthful and good. I had no difficulty in being so. My father gave me an example of a sincerity carried even to scrupulousness; my mother, of a goodness rising to devotion the most heroic. My soul, which breathed only an atmosphere of goodness, could not produce anything ungenial. I was never forced to struggle either with myself or with any other person. Everything attracted me; nothing constrained me. The little which I was taught was presented to me as a recompense. My sole masters were my father and my mother. I saw them read, and I wished to read; I gazed at them writing, and I asked them to aid me to form my letters. All this was carried on amidst sports and in leisure moments, on their knees, in the garden, at the fireside of the saloon, and accompanied by smiles, by railleries, by caresses. I acquired a taste for it. I suggested, of my own accord, these short and amusing lessons. I thus learned everything, a little late, it is true, but without ever recollecting how I learned it, and without a brow ever being bent to induce me to learn. I advanced without being conscious of making progress. My thoughts, ever in communion with those of my mother, were developed as it were in hers, as I had received nourishment from her bosom, until the moment I was forcibly and unhappily torn from her, when about to enter my twelfth year, to live the putrid or at least the frozen life of college. A taste for reading had early taken possession of me. It was with difficulty my parents could find a sufficient number of books appropriate to my age to gratify my curiosity. These childish books soon ceased to satisfy me. I gazed with longing at the volumes which were ranged in some shelves in a little cabinet off the saloon; but my mother curbed me in this impatience for knowledge. She gave me books only by degrees, and even these she selected carefully. An abridgment of the Bible; the fables of La Fontaine, which appeared to me at once childish, false, and cruel and which I could never learn by heart; the works of Madame de Genlis; those of Berquin; passages from Fenelon and

Bernardin de St. Pierre, which delighted me at that age; the Jerusalem delivered; Robinson Crusoe; some tragedies of Voltaire, especially Merope, read aloud by my father in the evening — it was from these that I drank in, as a plant from the soil, the first nourishing juices of my young intellect. But I drank deep, above all, from my mother's mind, I read through her eyes; I felt through her impressions; I lived through her life. She translated all for me — nature, sentiment, sensations, and thoughts. Without her I could not have spelled a line of that creation which I had before my eyes. But she guided my fingers over its page. Her soul was so luminous, so highly colored, and so warm, that she left a shadow or a chill on nothing. In leading me little by little to comprehend all, she made me at the same time love all. In a word, the insensible instruction which I received was not a lesson, it was the very act of living, of thinking, and of feeling which I accomplished before her eyes, along with her, like her, and through her. We lived a double life. It was thus that my heart was formed within me, on a model which I had not even the trouble of looking at, so closely was it blended with my own.

My mother displayed little anxiety about what is generally called instruction. She did not aspire to make me a child far advanced for my age. She did not arouse within me that emulation which is only the jealousy or the pride of children. She did not compare me to any person. She neither exalted nor humiliated me, by any dangerous comparisons. She thought, and justly, that once my intellectual strength

was developed by age, and by health of body and of
mind, I should learn as easily as others the little Greek
and Latin, and figures, of which is composed that
empty modicum of letters, which is called an educa-
tion.   What she wished was to make me a happy child,
with a healthy mind, and a loving soul; a creature of
God, and not a puppet of men.   She had drawn her
ideas upon education, at first from her own heart, and
then from the works of J. J. Rousseau and Bernardin
St. Pierre, those two favorite philosophers of women,
because they are the philosophers of feeling.   She
had become acquainted with, or caught a glimpse of,
both of them, in her childhood, at her mother's house.
She had subsequently read them and admired them.
She had heard, while still very young, their systems
debated a thousand times, by Madame de Genlis, and
by the skillful persons who were charged with the edu-
cation of the children of the Duke of Orleans.   It is
generally known that this prince was the first who ven-
tured to apply the theories of these natural philosophers
to the education of his sons.   My mother, brought
up along with them, and almost in the same manner
as they, naturally transferred these traditions of her
childhood to her own children.   She did so, how-
ever, carefully and with discernment.   She did not
confound what is suitable to be taught to princes,
placed by their birth and their wealth at the summit
of the social scale, with that which is suitable to be
taught to the children of a poor and obscure family,
placed close to the scenes of nature, in the modest
condition of labor and simplicity.   But what she

thought was that in all conditions of life, it is necessary first to make a man, and when the man is made — that is to say, a being intelligent, sensible, and placed in just relations to himself, to other men, and to God — it matters little whether he be a prince or a workman, he is that which he ought to be.   What he is, is good, and his mother's work is accomplished.

* *By permission of Harper & Brothers.*

MY MOTHER *

By Joseph Parker

And the sweet mother! So quiet, so patient, so full of hope.   Seeing everything without looking, praying much, and teaching her son to pray.   My wont was to sit near her with paper and pencil in hand, and to beg her to make one line of a hymn that I might try to add three lines to it.   No excitement known to boys was equal to that high joy.   One verse struck awe into the minds of my neighbors, and made them look at me with pride touched with reverence.   That verse was shown to the minister, and he, in excess of pastoral zeal, made rash predictions concerning the rhymester.   The father said nothing, but ordered it to be kept and shown to every visitor, and every visitor rose or fell in his estimation according to the view taken of that particular verse.   All the neighbors heard it and one said it ought to be put in a hymn-book; another was worldly enough to "bet" that some day I would make a whole hymn; others were struck dumb with amazement, only hinting that they who lived longest would see most.

Sweet mother! A sort of superstitious woman withal, and not indisposed to believe in ghosts. She was never quite comfortable without a twig of rowan tree in the house, and could never comfortably begin anything new on a Friday. How glad too, the dear soul was when she had a good " first-foot " on New Year's morning, for that " foot " mysteriously hinted at the character and fortune of the whole year. When she and I were in special perplexity she would take a Bible, pray briefly, open it, and according to the passage which was next her right-hand thumb, she would interpret the will of Heaven. This, she said, was the habit of the good John Wesley, and what Wesley did was right. I cannot despise those traits of character, for they point to something deeper than themselves, and in my mother's case they pointed to a character of extraordinary depth and religiousness.

* By permission of Funk & Wagnalls, from " My Life and Teaching."

CORNELIA AND HER JEWELS

By E. M. Sewall

Tiberius and Caius Gracchus were the grandsons of the first Scipio Africanus, the rival of Hannibal. Their mother, Cornelia, was his daughter. She was a very remarkable person, good and clever, as well as beautiful and elegant. Her daughter Semphronia married Scipio Æmilianus.

Cornelia took great pains to educate her children well, and as they grew up she became very proud of them. A lady one day came to pay her a visit, who was dressed very splendidly, and wore a great many jewels. Whilst they were talking together, she begged Cornelia to show her some of her ornaments. Cornelia sent for her sons, and when they appeared, she said, "These are my jewels, and their virtues are my ornaments." She had indeed much cause for satisfaction. Her sons were honorable, kind-hearted, handsome, and engaging. Their father had been famous for his uprightness and benevolence, and they were like him, especially Tiberius, the elder, who always took the part of oppressed persons, and was particularly desirous that the Romans should be less luxurious, and more strict in their manners and customs. His mother, we are told, thought so much of his talents and power, that she persuaded him to offer himself as a tribune of the people. "I am commonly called," she said, "by way of honor, the mother-in-law of the second Africanus. Why do they not call me the mother of the Gracchi?" She lived to have her wish fulfilled, but it brought her sorrow and desolation for the remainder of her days.

THE MOTHER OF THE GRACCHI

From Plutarch's Lives

Tiberius Gracchus, the grandson of Publius Sempronius and the father of Tiberius and Caius Grac-

chus; who, though he was once honored with the censorship, twice with the consulate, and led up two triumphs, yet derived still greater dignity from his virtues. Hence after the death of that Scipio who conquered Hannibal, he was thought worthy to marry Cornelia, the daughter of that great man. Cicero, in his first book *de Divinatione,* passes the highest encomiums on his virtue and wisdom and relates this story:—
It is said that he once caught a pair of serpents upon his bed, and that the soothsayers, after they had considered the prodigy, advised him neither to kill them both, nor let them both go. If he killed the male serpent, they told him his death would be the consequence; if the female, that of Cornelia. Tiberius who loved his wife, and thought it more suitable for him to die first, who was much older than his wife, killed the male, and set the female at liberty. Not long after this, he died, leaving Cornelia with no fewer than twelve children.

The care of the house and the children now entirely devolved on Cornelia; and she behaved with such sobriety, so much parental affection and greatness of mind, that Tiberius seems not to have judged ill, in choosing to die for so valuable a woman. For though Ptolemy, king of Egypt, paid his addresses to her, and offered her a share in his throne, she refused him. During her widowhood, she lost all her children except three, one daughter, who was married to Scipio the younger, and two sons Tiberius and Caius. Cornelia brought them up with so much care, that though they were without dispute of the noblest family, and had the happiest genius and disposition of all the Roman youth, yet education was allowed to have contributed more to their perfections than nature.

.   .   .   .

In a little time those commons showed how deeply they regretted the Gracchi. They erected their statues in one of the most public parts of the city; they consecrated the places where they were killed, and offered to them all first-fruits according to the season of the year. Nay, many offered daily sacrifices, and paid their devotions there as in the temples of the gods.

Cornelia is reported to have borne all these misfortunes with a noble magnanimity, and to have said of the consecrated places in particular, where her sons had lost their lives, "That they were monuments worthy of them." She took up her residence at Misenum, and made no alteration in her manner of living. As she had many friends, her table was always open for the purposes of hospitality. Greeks and other men of letters she had always with her, and all the kings in alliance with Rome expressed their regard by sending her presents, and receiving the like civilities in return. She made herself very agreeable to her guests by acquainting them with many particulars of her father Africanus, and of his manner of living. But what they most admired in her was, that she could recount their actions and sufferings, as if she spoke of her sons without a sigh or a tear, and had been giving a narrative of some ancient heroes. Some, therefore, imagined that age and the greatness of her misfortunes had deprived her of understanding and sensibility.

But those who were of that opinion seem rather to have wanted understanding themselves: since they knew not how much a noble mind may, by a liberal education, be enabled to support itself against distress: and that though in the pursuit of rectitude Fortune may often defeat the purposes of Virtue, yet Virtue, in bearing affliction, can never lose her prerogative.

The people honored Cornelia, not only on account of her children, but of her father. They afterwards erected a statue to her with this inscription:

CORNELIA THE MOTHER OF THE GRACCHI

MOTHERHOOD *

By Agnes Lee

Mother of Christ long slain, forth glided she,
   Following the children joyously astir
Under the cedars and the olive-tree,
   Pausing to let their laughter float to her.
Each voice an echo of a voice more dear,
   She saw a little Christ in every face.
When lo! another woman, passing near,
   Yearned o'er the tender life that filled the place,
And Mary sought the woman's hand, and said:
   " I know thee not, yet know thee memory-tossed
And what hath led thee here, as I am led —
   These bring to thee a child beloved and lost."

     " How radiant was my little one!
      And He was fair,
    Yea fairer than the fairest sun,

And like its rays through amber spun
   His sun-bright hair,
Still, I can see it shine and shine!"
 "Even so," the woman said, "was mine."

 "His ways were ever darling ways,"
   And Mary smiled,—
"So soft and clinging! Glad relays
Of love were all his precious days —
   My little child
Was like an infinite that gleamed."
"Even so was mine," the woman dreamed.

Then whispered Mary: "Tell me, thou
   Of thine!" And she:
"Oh, mine was rosy as a bough
Blooming with roses, sent, somehow,
   To bloom for me!
His balmy fingers left a thrill
Within my breast that warms me still."

Then gazed she down some wilder, darker hour
And said, when Mary questioned knowing not:
 "Who art thou, mother of so sweet a flower?"
  "I am the mother of Iscariot."

   * By permission of "The North American Review." Issue of October, 1907.

THE MOTHER OF EMERSON

By George Willis Cooke

Ralph Waldo Emerson was born in Boston, in 1803. His father died before he was eight years old, leaving five sons,— William, Ralph Waldo, Edward Bliss, Peter Bulkeley, and Charles Chauncy. His mother, Ruth Haskins, was a woman of great sensibility, modest, serene, and very devout. She was possessed of a thoroughly sincere nature, devoid of all sentimentalism, and of a temper the most even and placid. One of her sons said, that, in his boyhood, when she came from her room in the morning, it seemed to him as if she always came from communion with God. She has been described as possessed of " great patience and fortitude, of the serenest trust in God, of a discerning spirit, and a most courteous bearing, one who knew how to guide the affairs of her own house, as long as she was responsible for that, with the sweetest authority, and knew how to give the least trouble and the greatest happiness after that authority was resigned. Both her mind and character were of a superior order, and they set their stamp upon manners of peculiar softness and natural grace and quiet dignity. Her sensible and kindly speech was always as good as the best instruction; her smile, though it was ever ready, was a reward. Her dark liquid eyes, from which old age could not take away the expression, will be among the remembrances of all on whom they ever rested."

During the boyhood of her sons, Mrs. Emerson found a faithful helper in her husband's sister, Miss Mary Emerson. This aunt was also a woman of many remarkable qualities, high-toned in motive and conduct to the largest degree, very conscientious and with an unconventional disregard of social forms.

Waldo was greatly indebted to her. He once declared her influence upon his education to have been as great as that of Greece or Rome, and he described her as a great genius and a remarkable writer.

In this pious and conscientious household, where the most careful economy was practiced, Waldo Emerson grew up to the strictest regard for all that is good and true. The mother and the aunt exercised a rare influence over him and his brothers. Honesty, probity and unselfishness — these virtues they had deeply instilled into them. In after years Waldo was once asked if he had read a certain novel; and he replied that he had once, in his boyhood, taken it from a circulating library, paying six cents for the use of the first volume. His aunt chided him for spending money in that way, when it was so hard for his mother to obtain it. He was so affected by this appeal he returned the volume, but did not take out the other. His remembrance of this incident had prevented his ever completing the book he had so much enjoyed until this appeal was made to his sense of duty.

THE MOTHER OF BRYANT *

By Parke Godwin

Sarah Snell, the mother of the poet, was a woman of vigorous understanding and energetic character. Having gone to a new settlement when she was only six years old, she had enjoyed few of the advantages of education; but as her youngest son writes: "Amidst the hardships and privations incident to a life in the forest, she grew up to a stately womanhood. Her opportunities were necessarily limited, so far as schools and books were concerned, but she made a creditable progress in all the rudimentary branches of learning." Her household activity and diligence would, in this latter age of the world, be considered something marvelous. In the days of general impoverishment after the war, the mother of the household did nearly all her own domestic work. Factories there were none, and, if there had been any, the roads were too rough to render them of much avail. Each family had its own spinning-wheels — a smaller one in the corner of the sitting-room, to which the busy foot of the matron was applied in the long winter evenings, and the larger one in the hall or garret, where she could walk back and forth with the spindle in her hands, and twist the clean flax or tow into threads. It had also its loom for the weaving of cloth, its carpet-frames, its candle-molds, and its dye-pots for the coloring of fabrics from the extracts of various woods and weeds. Mrs. Bryant performed all these labors. An idea of the amount of them is obtained from the little diary, in which she registered what was done from day to day while she was surrounded by her young children. It is filled with such items as these: "Made Austin a coat"; "Spun four skeins of tow"; "Spun thirty knots of linen"; "Taught Cullen his letters"; "Made a pair of breeches "; " Wove four yards and went a-quilting "; " Made a dress for the boy "; " Sewed on a shirt "; " Wove four yards and visited Mrs.———"; " Washed and ironed "; " Spun and wove "; And so the simple record runs on year after year.

" All this work our mother did," says John Bryant, with pardonable pride, " looking after her children, feeding them and nursing them in sickness, teaching them to read and write, which was faithfully attended to during their earlier years, while she turned the wheel by the winter fire. In those times many shifts and expedients of economy were necessary to maintain an honorable independence, which are rarely thought of in these days, even by the poorest people. Not only was she industrious and persevering in ordinary labor, but she took a deep interest in public affairs, both national and State, never neglecting any of her house duties, but visiting constantly, especially the sick, whom she nursed for days and nights together. She exerted a considerable influence in township and neighborhood improvements, such as schools, roads, etc. It was through her persuasion with us boys that the maple and other shade trees were planted around the homestead and along the highways. Having observed something of the kind when on a journey, she resolved as soon as she returned to have a similar work done at home. These were the first trees set by the roadside in all that region, where thousands have since been planted. She discouraged all bad habits in her household, such as drinking, tobacco chewing and smoking, and idleness and profanity. From this last vice I believe all her children were entirely free, for if any of them ever uttered an oath, I never heard of it. I have often heard her exclaim, ' Above all things, I abhor drunkenness ! ' also ' Never be idle; always be doing something '; ' If you are never idle, you will find time for everything.' "

As there were no large schools in the vicinity, the Bryant children were mainly educated by the efforts of their parents. In the spring and summer the young men, as they grew to be old enough, took part in the labors of the farm, and the young women at all seasons in those of the household; but the long winter evenings were given by both to study. Dr. Bryant was something of a scholar, knowing the Greek, Latin, and French languages, and possessing, in addition to the largest medical library in those parts, a considerable number of the more important works of English literature, especially of the poets, having been himself addicted to making verses.

Another son writing of his mother's strength says: " When my mother came to Illinois in 1835, she said, at the house of my brother Cyrus, that she used when young, to mount a horse from the ground. He affecting incredulity, remarked that he should like to see it done, when she, piqued by his apparent scepticism, added that if a horse was brought to the door she would do it again. A horse was saddled and brought to the door, and, though she was sixty-seven years old, she performed the feat."

* From " The Life of William Cullen Bryant." D. Appleton Company.

OLIVER CROMWELL'S MOTHER

By William M. Thayer

From *Turning Points in Successful Careers*

" There is a picture of this excellent woman still preserved at Hitchinbrook, which represents her to be a person somewhat above middle height, and having large, pensive eyes, a finely chiseled mouth, and clear lustrous forehead, mantled with bright hair; the whole countenance lit up and harmonized by the sweetest expression imaginable. Oliver loved and honored this admirable mother, and was in return tenderly beloved by her; and this fact alone might sufficiently refute much of the calumny heaped upon his youth."

Oliver was a bold, rough, adventurous boy, full of spirit and purpose. Some of his neighbors said he was pugnacious and naughty, inclined to join bad boys in raids on orchards and melon-patches. But his parents held him with a tight rein, and chastised him severely for pranks and disobedience. . . . Oliver's mother was a deeply pious woman, and she managed him as a truly Christian mother. She made him familiar with the Bible in very early life, so that he understood perfectly well his duties to God and man. He was inducted into the church in his youth, a fact that indicated he was thoughtful, exemplary, and desirous of living for God. All through his life he was noted for his acquaintance with the Scriptures. He was able to repeat whole chapters and even books.

This fact indicates the thoroughness of maternal lessons. He was established in religious truth at the fireside. And this was the influence that kept his reckless nature from rushing to ruin. . . .

His mother was living when Oliver became Protector, and she dwelt with him in Whitehall Palace. Every day he visited her room, and affectionately inquired after her health, exchanging with her words of endearment. She died at the age of ninety-four, in full possession of her faculties. Oliver stood by her bedside in tears. Looking up, she said, " My dear son, I leave my heart with thee; good-night." These were her last words. With the tender memories of a grateful son, Cromwell laid her body away in Westminster Abbey with the honored dead of his country.

THE MOTHER OF CAIUS MARCIUS CORIOLANUS

From Plutarch's Lives

When Valeria had thus spoken, the rest of the women joined her request. Volumnia gave them this answer: " Besides the share which we have in the general calamity, we are, my friends, in particular, very unhappy; since Marcius is lost to us, his glory obscured, and his virtue gone; since we behold him surrounded by the arms of the enemies of his country, not as their prisoner, but their commander. But it is still a greater misfortune to us, if our country is become so weak as to have need to repose her hopes upon us.

For I know not whether he will have any regard for us, since he has had none for his country, which he used to prefer to his mother, to his wife, and children. Take us, however, and make what use of us you please. Lead us to him. If we can do nothing else, we can expire at his feet in supplicating for Rome."

She then took the children and Virgilia with her, and went with the other matrons to the Volscian camp. The sight of them produced, even in the enemy, compassion and a reverential silence. Coriolanus, who then happened to be seated upon the tribunal with his principal officers, seeing the women approach, was greatly agitated and surprised. Nevertheless, he endeavored to retain his wonted sternness and inexorable temper, though he perceived that his wife was at the head of them. But, unable to resist the emotions of affection, he could not suffer them to address him as he sat. He descended from the tribunal and ran to meet them. First he embraced his mother for a considerable time, and afterwards his wife and children, neither refraining from tears nor any other instance of natural tenderness.

When he had sufficiently indulged his passion, and perceived that his mother wanted to speak, he called the Volscian counselors to him, and Volumnia expressed herself to this purpose: " You see, my son, by our attire and miserable looks, and therefore I may spare myself the trouble of declaring, to what condition your banishment has reduced us. Think with yourself whether we are not the most unhappy of women, when fortune has changed the spectacle that should have been the most pleasing in the world, into the most dreadful; when Volumnia beholds her son, and Virgilia her husband, encamped in a hostile manner before the walls of his native city. And what to others is the greatest consolation under misfortune and adversity, I mean prayer to the gods, to us is rendered impracticable: for we cannot at the same time beg victory for our country and your preservation, but what our worst enemies would imprecate on us a curse, must of necessity be interwoven with our prayers. Your wife and children must either see their country perish, or you. As to my own part, I will not live to see this war decided by fortune. If I cannot persuade you to prefer friendship and union, to enmity and its ruinous consequences, and so to become the benefactor to both sides, rather than the destruction of one, you must take this along with you, and prepare to expect it, that you shall not advance against your country, without trampling upon the dead body of her that bore you. For it does not become me to wait for that day, when my son shall be either led captive by his fellow-citizens, or triumph over Rome. If, indeed, I desired you to save your country by ruining the Volscians I confess the case would be hard, and the choice difficult: for it would neither be honorable to destroy your countrymen, nor just to betray those who have placed their confidence in you. But what do we desire of you, more than deliverance from our own calamities? A deliverance which will be equally salutary to both parties, but most to the honor of the Volscians, since it will appear that their superiority empowered them to grant us the greatest of blessings, peace and friendship, while they themselves receive the same. If these take place, you will be acknowledged to be the principal cause of them: if they do not, you alone must expect to bear the blame from both nations. And though the chance of war is uncertain, yet it will be the certain event of this, that if you conquer, you will be a destroying demon to your country: if you are beaten, it will be clear that, by indulging your resentment, you have plunged your friends and benefactors in the greatest of misfortunes."

Coriolanus listened to his mother while she went on with her speech, without saying the least word to her: and Volumnia, seeing him stand a long time mute after she had left speaking, proceeded again in this manner: "Why are you silent, my son? Is it an honor to yield everything to anger and resentment, and would it be a disgrace to yield to your mother in so important a petition? Or does it become a great man to remember the injuries done him, and would it not equally become a great and good man, with the highest regard and reverence, to keep in mind the benefits he has received from his parents? Surely you of all men, should take care to be grateful, who have suffered so extremely by ingratitude. And yet, though you have already severely punished your country, you have not made your mother the least return for her kindness. The most sacred ties both of nature and religion, without other constraint, require that you should indulge me in this just and reasonable request: but if words cannot prevail, this only resource is left." When she had said this, she threw herself at his feet, together with his wife and children: upon which Coriolanus crying out, "O mother! what is it you have done?" raised her from the ground, and tenderly pressing her hand, continued, "You have gained a victory fortunate for your country, but ruinous to me. I go, vanquished by you alone." Then, after a short conference with his mother and wife in private, he sent them back to Rome, agreeably to their desire. Next morning he drew off the Volscians, who had not all the same sentiments of what had passed. Some blamed him, others, whose inclinations were for peace, found no fault: others again, though they disliked what was done, did not look upon Coriolanus as a bad man, but thought he was excusable in yielding to such powerful solicitations. However, none presumed to contradict his orders, though they followed him rather out of veneration for his virtue, than regard to his authority.

MY IDEA OF MY MOTHER

BY COUNT TOLSTOY

"My mother I do not at all remember. I was a year and a half old when she died. Owing to some strange chance no portrait of her has been preserved, so that, as a real physical being, I cannot represent her to myself. I am in a sense glad of this, for in my conception of her there is only her spiritual figure, and all that I know about her is beautiful, and I think this is so, not only because all who spoke to me of my mother tried to say only what was good, but because there was actually very much of this good in her. . . .

" My mother was not handsome. She was well educated for her time. Besides Russian, which, contrary to the national illiterateness then current, she wrote correctly, she knew four other languages, French, German, English, and Italian, and was probably sensitive to art. She played well on the piano, and her friends have told me that she was a great hand at narrating most attractive tales invented at the moment. . . .

" I have preserved several of her letters to my father and aunts, and her diary concerning the conduct of Nikolenka (my eldest brother) who was six years old when she died, and I think resembled her more than the rest of us. They both possessed a feature very dear to me, which I infer from my mother's letters, but personally witnessed in my brother : their indifference to the opinion of others, and their modesty in their endeavors to conceal those mental, educational, and moral advantages which they had in comparison with others. They were, as it were, ashamed of these advantages.

" I remark the same feature in my mother's letters. She evidently stood on a higher level than my father and his family, with the exception, perhaps, of Tatiana Yergolsky, with whom I passed half my life, and who was a woman remarkable for her moral qualities.

" Besides this, they both had yet another feature which I believe contributed to their indifference to the judgment of men — it was that they never condemned any one.

" A feature which distinguishes my mother among her circle was her truthfulness and the simple tone of her letters. At that time the expression of exaggerated feelings was especially cultivated in letters : ' Incomparable, divine, the joy of my life, unutterably precious,' etc., were the most usual epithets between friends, and the more inflated the less sincere.

" I have been told that my mother loved me very much, and called me ' Mon petit Benjamin ' . . .

". . . The fourth strong feeling which did perhaps exist, as my aunts told me — I earnestly hope that it did exist — was her love for me, which took the place of her love for Koko, who at the time of my birth had already detached himself from his mother and been transferred into male hands. It was a necessity for her to love what was not herself, and one love took the place of another.

" Such was the figure of my mother in my imagination. She appeared to me a creature so elevated, pure, and spiritual that often in the middle period of my life, during my struggle with overwhelming temptations, I prayed to her soul, begging her to aid me, and this prayer always helped me much.

" My mother's life in her father's family was a very good and happy one, as I may conclude from letters and stories.

" My father's household consisted of his mother,

an old lady; of her daughter, my aunt Countess Alexandra Osten-Saken, and her ward Pashenka; of another aunt, as we used to call her, although she was a very distant relative, Tatiana Yergolsky, who had been educated in my grandfather's house and had passed all her later life in my father's; and the tutor, Feodor Ivanovich Resselier. We were five children — Nicolay, Sergey, Dmitri, myself, the youngest boy, and our younger sister Mashenka, at whose birth my mother died. My mother's very short married life — I think it lasted not more than nine years — was very full, and adorned by every one's love to her and hers to every one who lived with her. Judging by the letters, I see that she lived at that time in great solitude. Scarcely anyone visited Yasnaya Polmana except our intimate friends the Ogarefs and some relatives who, if casually traveling along the high-road, might look in upon them.

" My mother's life was passed in occupations with the children, in reading aloud of an evening to my grandmother, and in serious readings such as Emile, by Rousseau and discussions about what had been read; in playing the piano, teaching Italian to one of my aunts, walks, and household work. In all families there are periods when illness and death are yet unknown, and the members live peacefully. Such a period, it seems to me, my mother was living through in her husband's family until her death. No one died, no one was seriously ill, my father's disordered affairs were improving. All were healthy, happy, and friendly. My father amused every one with his stories and jokes. I did not witness that time. At the time with which my remembrances begin, my mother's death had already laid its seal upon the life of our family. All this I have described from what I have heard and from letters."

THE MOTHER OF CARLYLE *

By James Froude

The strongest personal passion which he (Carlyle) experienced through all his life was his affection for his mother. She was proud and willful as he. He had sent or offered her, more presents, and she had been angry with him. She had not been well, and she was impatient of doctors' regulations.

Birmingham, August 29, 1824.

To Mrs. Carlyle, Mainhill.

I must suggest some improvements in your diet and mode of life which might be of service to *you,* who I know too well have much to suffer on your own part, though your affection renders you so exclusively anxious about me. You will say you cannot be *fashed.* Oh, my dear mother, if you did not think of what value your health and comfort are to us all, you would never talk so. Are we not all bound to you, by sacred and indissoluble ties? Am I not so bound more than any other? Who was it that nursed me and watched me in frowardness and sickness from the earliest dawn of my existence to this hour? — My mother. Who is it that has struggled for me in pain and sorrow with undespairing diligence, that has for me been up early and down late, caring for me, laboring for me, unweariedly assisting me? — My mother. Who is the one that never shrunk from me in my desolation, that never tired of my despondencies, or shut up by a look or tone of impatience the expression of my real or imaginary griefs? Who is it that loves me and will love me for ever with an affection which no chance, no misery, no crime of mine can do away? — It is you, my mother. As the greatest favor that I can beg of you, let me, now that I have in some degree the power, be of some assistance in promoting your comfort. It were one of the achievements which I could look back upon with most satisfaction from all the stages of my earthly pilgrimage, if I could make you happier. Are we not all of us animated by a similar love to you? Why then will you spare any trouble, any cost, in what is valuable beyond aught earthly to every one of us?

By permission of Charles Scribner's Sons.

WHAT MOTHERS HAVE DONE

" All that I am or hope to be," said Lincoln, after he became President of the United States, " I owe to my angel mother."

" All that I have ever accomplished in life," declared Dwight L. Moody, the great evangelist, " I owe to my mother."

" To the man who has had a mother, all women are sacred for her sake," said Jean Paul Richter.

"A kiss from my mother made me a painter," said Benjamin West.

MONICA, ST. AUGUSTINE'S MOTHER

In his book *de Beata Vita,* Augustine thus addresses his mother: "You, through whose prayers I undoubtedly believe and affirm, that God gave me that mind that I should prefer nothing to the discovery of truth; wish, think of, love, nought besides. Nor do I fail to believe, that this so great good, which, through thee, I have come to desire, through thy prayers I shall attain;"

And says of her, "chiefly my mother, to whom I believe, I owe all which in me is life," and long after, "that to the faithful and daily tears of my mother, I was granted, that I should not perish."

And again, he says: "Our mother, whose endowments, and the fervor of her mind towards divine things, I had both before perceived through daily intercourse and careful observation, and in a discussion on a matter of no small moment, her mind had appeared of so high an order, that nothing could be more adapted to the study of true wisdom."

Augustine speaks of her "ardent love of the divine Scriptures" and preserves an answer of hers as to what constituted happiness, "If a man desire what is good and has it, he is happy; if evil, though he have it, he is wretched."

This from his Confessions: "We sought where we might serve Thee most usefully, and were together returning to Africa; witherward being as far as Ostia, my mother departed this life. . . .

"The day now approaching whereon she was to depart this life, (which day Thou well knewest, we knew not,) it came to pass, Thyself, as I believe, by Thy secret ways so ordering it, that she and I stood alone, leaning in a certain window, which looked into the garden of the house where we now lay, at Ostia; where removed from the din of men, we were recruiting from the fatigues of a long journey, for the voyage. We were discoursing then together, alone, very sweetly; and *forgetting those things which are behind, and reaching forth unto those things which are before,* we were enquiring between ourselves in the presence of the Truth, which Thou art, of what sort the eternal life of the saints was to be, *which eye hath not seen, nor ear heard, nor hath it entered into the heart of man.* . . .

"When we were speaking of these things, and this world with all its delights became, as we spake, contemptible to us, my mother said, 'Son, for my own part I have no further delight in anything in this life. What I do here any longer, and to what end I am here, I know not, now that my hopes in this world are accomplished. One thing there was, for which I desired to linger for a while in this life, that I might see thee a Catholic Christian before I died. My God hath done this for me more abundantly, that I should now see thee withal, despising earthly happiness, become His servant: what do I here?'

"What answer I made her unto these things, I remember not. For scarce five days after, or not much more, she fell sick of a fever. . . .

"On the ninth day then of her sickness, and the fifty-sixth of her age, and the three and thirtieth of mine, was that religious and holy soul freed from the body. I closed her eyes; and there flowed withal a mighty sorrow in my heart. . . .

"What then was it which did grievous pain me within, but a fresh wound wrought through the sudden wrench of that most sweet and dear custom of living together? I joyed indeed in her testimony, when, in her last sickness, mingling her endearments with my acts of duty, she called me 'dutiful,' and mentioned with great affection of love, that she never had heard any harsh or reproachful sound uttered by my mouth against her. But yet, O my God, Who madest us, what comparison is there betwixt that honor that I paid to her, and her slavery for me? Being then forsaken of so great comfort in her, my soul was wounded, and that life rent asunder as it were, which, of hers and mine together, had been made but one."

"Together 'neath the Italian heaven
They sit, the mother and her son,
He late from her by errors riven,
Now both in Jesus one:
The dear consenting hands are knit,
And either face, as there they sit,
Is lifted as to something seen
Beyond the blue serene."

In an epitaph of Bassus, ex-consul, dating from the fifth century, Monica is addressed as the " Mother of Virtues " and Augustine as her yet happier offspring. This shows the early reverence paid to her memory.

Monica is a saint in the Roman Calendar, April Fourth. Her bones were translated from Ostia to Rome in 1480 under Pope Martin V. and deposited in a chapel dedicated to Augustine.

VII

LULLABIES

AT SINGING TIME *

By ANNE P. L. FIELD

I have a little daughter
  Who's scarcely half-past three
And in the twilight hour
  She climbs upon my knee
And snuggles down within my arm
  With " Mother, sing to me!"

I sing about the squirrels
  That frolic in the wood,
About two furry kittens —
  One naughty and one good
And then some tender lullabies —
  Just as a mother should.

The light grows faint, and fainter;
  The sandman guards the door;
My baby's boat drifts slowly
  Upon the slumber shore —
But if the singing stops, she cries,
  " O Mother, sing some more!"

I'm sure no prima-donna
  Adored from East to West,

Feels half the satisfaction,
　Or is so truly blest
As I, when singing to my child
　Held closely to my breast.

Not all the fame and glory
　Of divas can compare
With that deep thrill of pleasure
　Which is my humble share,
For precious are the laurel-wreaths
　That singing-mothers wear!

By permission of " The Independent."

JAPANESE LULLABY *

By Eugene Field

Sleep, little pigeon, and fold your wings,—
　Little blue pigeon with velvet eyes;
Sleep to the singing of mother-bird swinging —
　Swinging the nest where her little one lies.

Away out yonder I see a star,—
　Silvery star with a tinkling song;
To the soft dew falling I hear it calling —
　Calling and tinkling the night along.

In through the window a moonbeam comes,—
　Little gold moonbeam with misty wings;
All silently creeping, it asks: " Is he sleeping —
　Sleeping and dreaming while mother sings?"

Up from the sea there floats the sob
  Of the waves that are breaking upon the shore,
As though they were groaning in anguish, and moan-
      ing —
  Bemoaning the ship that shall come no more.

But sleep, little pigeon, and fold your wings,—
  Little blue pigeon with mournful eyes;
Am I not singing? — see, I am swinging —
  Swinging the nest where my darling lies.

* By permission of Charles Scribner's Sons.

CRADLE SONG

By Thomas Bailey Aldrich

Ere the moon begins to rise
    Or a star to shine,
All the blue bells close their eyes —
    So close thine,
        Thine, dear, thine!

Birds are sleeping in the nest
    On the swaying bough,
Thus, against the mother-breast —
    So sleep thou,
        Sleep, sleep, thou!

GO SLEEP, MA HONEY

By Edward D. Barker

Whipp'will's singin' to de moon,—
    Go sleep, ma honey, m — m.

He sing a pow'ful mo'nful tune,
    Go sleep, ma honey, m — m.
De day bird's sleepin' on his nes',
He know it time to take a res',
An' he gwine ter do his lebel bes',
    Go sleep, ma honey, m — m.

Old banjo's laid away,—
    Go sleep, ma honey, m — m.
It's pickin's froo for to-day,—
    Go sleep, ma honey, m — m.
De night time surely come to pass,
De cricket's chirpin' in de grass,
An' de ole mule's gone to sleep at las',—
    Go sleep, ma honey, m — m.

I hear de night win' in de corn,—
    Go sleep, ma honey, m — m.
Dey's a ghos' out dah, sure's yo born,—
    Go sleep, ma honey, m — m.
But he dassent come where we keep a light,
An' de candle's burnin' all de night,
So sink to res', des be all right,—
    Go sleep, ma honey, m — m.

A SUMMER LULLABY

By E. S. Bumstead

The sun has gone from the shining skies;
    Bye, baby, bye,

The dandelions have closed their eyes;
      Bye, baby, bye,
And the stars are lighting their lamps to see
If the babies and squirrels and birds, all three,
Are sound asleep as they ought to be.
      Bye, baby, bye.

The squirrel is dressed in a coat of gray;
      Bye, baby, bye,
He wears it by night as well as by day;
      Bye, baby, bye,
The robin sleeps in his feathers and down,
With the warm red breast and the wings of brown;
But the baby wears a little white gown.
      Bye, baby, bye.

The squirrel's nest is a hole in a tree;
      Bye, baby, bye,
And there he sleeps as snug as can be;
      Bye, baby, bye,
The robin's nest is high overhead,
Where the leafy boughs of the maple spread,
But the baby's nest is a little white bed.
      Bye, baby, bye.

CRADLE-SONG OF THE FISHERMAN'S WIFE

By Ella Higginson

Swung in the hollows of the deep,
While silver stars their watches keep,
    Sleep, my seabird, sleep!

Our boat the glistening fishes fill,
Our prow turns homeward — hush be still,
   Sleep, my seabird, sleep —
     Sleep, sleep.

The wind is springing from out the West,
Nestle thee deeper in mother's breast,
   Rest, my seabird, rest!
There is no sea our boat can whelm
While thy brave father is at the helm,
   Rest, my seabird, rest —
     Rest, rest.

The foam flies past us, the lightnings gleam,
The waves break over, the fierce winds scream
   Dream, my seabird, dream!
Dream of the cot where high and low,
Crimson and white, the roses blow,
   Dream, my seabird, dream —
     Dream, dream.

What though the tempest is on the deep?
Heaven will guard thee — do not weep,
   Sleep, my seabird, sleep!
Be brave as a fisherman's child should be,
Rocked in the hollows of the sea,
   Sleep, my seabird, sleep —
     Sleep, sleep.

LULLABY

By Alfred Tennyson

Sweet and low, sweet and low,
    Wind of the western sea,
Low, low, breathe and blow,
    Wind of the western sea!
Over the rolling waters go,
Come from the dying moon, and blow,
    Blow him again to me;
While my little one, while my pretty one, sleeps.

Sleep and rest, sleep and rest,
    Father will come to thee soon:
Rest, rest, on mother's breast,
    Father will come to thee soon;
Father will come to his bird in the nest;
Silver sails all out of the west
    Under the silver moon:
Sleep, my little one, sleep, my pretty one, sleep.

CRADLE SONG

Anonymous

Sleep, little baby of mine,
Night and the darkness are near,
But Jesus looks down
Through the shadows that frown,
And baby has nothing to fear.

Shut, little sleepy blue eyes;
Dear little head be at rest;
Jesus, like you,
Was a baby once, too,
And slept on his own mother's breast.

Sleep, little baby of mine,
Soft on your pillow so white;
Jesus is here
To watch over you, dear,
And nothing can harm you to-night.

O, little darling of mine,
What can you know of the bliss,
The comfort I keep,
Awake and asleep,
Because I am certain of this?

SWEETLY SLEEP

By Jane Taylor

Sleep, my baby; sleep, my boy;
  Rest your little weary head!
'Tis your mother rocks her boy
  In his little cradle-bed.
    Lullaby, sweet lullaby,
    Lullaby, sweet lullaby,
  In his little cradle-bed.

All the little birds are sleeping
  Every one has gone to rest;

And my precious one is resting
  In his pretty cradle nest.
    Lullaby, sweet lullaby,
    Lullaby, sweet lullaby,
  In his pretty cradle nest.

Sleep, oh, sleep, my darling boy —
  Wake to-morrow fresh and strong;
'Tis thy mother sits beside thee,
  Singing thee an evening song.
    Lullaby, sweet lullaby,
    Lullaby, sweet lullaby,
  Singing thee an evening song.

A CRADLE HYMN

By Isaac Watts

Hush! my dear, lie still, and slumber,
  Holy angels guard thy bed!
Heavenly blessings without number
  Gently falling on thy head.

Sleep, my babe; they food and raiment,
  House and home, thy friends provide;
All without thy care or payment
  All thy wants are well supplied.

How much better thou'rt attended
  Than the Son of God could be

When from heaven he descended,
    And became a child like thee.

Soft and easy is thy cradle:
    Coarse and hard thy Saviour lay:
When his birthplace was a stable,
    And his softest bed was hay.

See the kinder shepherds round him,
    Telling wonders from the sky!
There they sought him, there they found him,
    With his Virgin Mother by.

See the lovely babe a-dressing:
    Lovely infant how he smiled!
When he wept, the mother's blessing
    Soothed and hushed the holy Child.

Lo, he slumbers in his manger,
    Where the hornèd oxen feed;
Peace, my darling, here's no danger,
    Here's no ox anear thy bed.

Mayst thou live to know and fear him,
    Trust and love him all thy days;
Then go dwell forever near him,
    See his face and sing his praise!

I could give thee thousand kisses,
    Hoping what I most desire;
Not a mother's fondest wishes
    Can to greater joys aspire.

A NURSERY SONG

By Mrs. Carter

As I walked over the hills one day,
I listened and heard a mother-sheep say:
" In all the green world there is nothing so sweet
As my little lammie with his nimble feet,
　　　With his eyes so bright,
　　　And his wool so white,
　Oh, he is my darling, my heart's delight.
　　　The robin, he
　　　That sings in a tree,
Dearly may doat on his darlings four,
But I love my one little lambkin more,"
And the mother-sheep and her little one
Side by side lay down in the sun;
And they went to sleep on the hill-side warm,
While my little lammie lies here on my arm.

I went to the kitchen, and what did I see,
But the old gray cat with her kittens three;
I heard her whispering soft — said she:
" My kittens, with tails all so cunningly curled,
Are the prettiest things that can be in the world;
　　　The bird on the tree,
　　　And the old ewe she,
　May love their babies exceedingly;
　　　But I love my kittens there
　　　Under the rocking-chair,
　I love my kittens with all my might.

Which is the prettiest I cannot tell —
    Which of the three —
    For the life of me —
I love them all so well.
Now I'll take up my kitties, the kitties I love,
And we'll lie down together beneath the warm stove."
Let the kitties sleep under the stove so warm,
While my little darling lies here on my arm.

I went to the yard, and saw an old hen
Go clucking about with her chickens ten.
She clucked, and she scratched, and she bristled away,
And what do you think I heard her say?
I heard her say : " The sun never did shine
On anything like to these chickens of mine.
You may hunt the full moon and the stars, if you
        please,
But you never will find ten such chickens as these.
The cat loves her kittens, the ewe loves her lamb,
But they do not know what a proud mother I am ;
For lambs, nor for kittens, I won't part with these,
Tho' the sheep and the cats should go down on their
        knees ;
    No ! no ! not though
    The kittens could crow
Or the lammie on two yellow legs could go.
My dear, downy darlings ! my sweet little things !
Come nestle now, cosily, under my wing."
    So the hen said,
    And the chickens all sped
As fast as they could to their nice feather-bed,

And there let them sleep in their feathers so warm,
While my little chick nestles here on my arm.

SLEEP, BABY, SLEEP

ANONYMOUS

Sleep, baby, sleep!
Thy father watches the sheep;
Thy mother is shaking the dream-land tree,
And down falls a little dream on thee:
Sleep, baby, sleep!

Sleep, baby, sleep!
The large stars are the sheep,
The little stars are the lambs I guess,
The fair moon is the shepherdess:
Sleep, baby, sleep!

NOW LET ME LAY THE PEARL AWAY

BY E. PRENTISS

Now let me lay the pearl away,
That on my breast I've worn all day;
How sweet, how soft the casket fair,
Where hides all night my jewel rare.

My snow-white lamb, thy gambols o'er,
Thy sportive limbs must sport no more;
Now to thy rest, let slumber creep
With gentle tread to bid thee sleep.

My winsome one! my heart's delight!
I give thee to the arms of night;
O darksome night! with soft caress
My darling little baby bless.

My heart's delight! my pearl, my lamb!
How rich, how blest, how glad I am!
In sweetest sleep I see thee lie;
Good-bye, good-night! good-night, good-bye!

THE LULLABY OF DANÄE

By Edmund C. Stedman

Paraphrase on Simonides, 500 B.C.

Little one, thy mother's weeping;
　　Thou with fresh and holy heart
　　Slumbering on the ocean art; —
While I sorrow, thou art sleeping,
Though the pallor and the gloom
Our forlorn, frail bark entomb.
Rest thee, rest thee, little one!

Ah! thou needest not a pillow
　　With those tresses thick and fair!
Ah! thou heedest not a billow
　　Moistening thy tangled hair,
Nor the voices of the storm,
But in thy purple mantlet liest warm,
My beautiful, my own!
Rest thee, rest thee, pretty one!

Yet if pain were pain to thee,
  If thou knewest how to fear,
  And didst lend thy little ear,
I would say again to thee:
Rest thee, rest thee, darling one!

I would bid thee, baby, sleep;
And be thou hushed, O restless deep!
Thou, too, my boundless sorrow!
Father, let some fairer morrow
Change for us thy sovran will,
Bring us good beyond this ill!
When I make too bold a prayer,
Thy vengeance on the babe forbear,
Let my head receive it still!
Rest thee, rest thee, little one!

Note,— This lyrical fragment, preserved through twenty-four
centuries, possesses in the original Greek a tenderness and
melody of surpassing delicacy. The poet's theme is Danäe,
exposed with her infant (of whom her father had a supersti-
tious fear) in an open ark, or coffer, to the fury of the waves.
According to the poem, " When the wild winds beat upon the
wroughten ark, and the perturbed sea brought terror to her
soul, she threw her arms around Perseus, and sang: ' Little
one, thy mother's weeping! ' " etc.

A MOTHER'S EVENING HYMN

By Martin Luther

Translated by John Christian Jacobi (1722)

Sleep well, my dear, sleep safe and free;
The holy angels are with thee,

Who always see thy Father's face,
And never slumber nights nor days.

Thou liest in down, soft every way;
Thy Saviour lay in straw and hay;
Thy cradle is far better drest
Than the hard crib where He did rest.

God make thy mother's health increase,
To see thee grow in strength and grace,
In wisdom and humility,
As infant Jesus did for thee.

Sleep now, my dear, and take thy rest;
And if with riper years thou'rt blest,
Increase in wisdom, day and night,
Till thou attain'st th' eternal Light.

THE COTTAGER'S LULLABY

By Dorothy Wordsworth

The days are cold, the nights are long;
The north-wind sings a doleful song;
Then hush again upon my breast,
All merry things are now at rest,
  Save thee, my pretty love!

The kitten sleeps upon the hearth,
The crickets long have ceased their mirth;
There's nothing stirring in the house

Save one wee, hungry, nibbling mouse;
    Then why so busy thou?

Nay, start not at that sparkling light;
'Tis but the moon that shines so bright
On the window-pane bedropped with rain;
Then, little darling! sleep again,
    And wake when it is day.

SWEDISH MOTHER'S LULLABY

By Frederika Bremer

There sitteth a dove, so fair and white,
    All on a lily spray;
And she listeneth how to the Saviour above
    The little children pray.

Lightly she spreads her friendly wings,
    And to heaven's gate hath sped,
And unto the Father in heaven she bears
    The prayers the children have said.

And back she comes from heaven's gate,
    And brings — that dove so mild —
From the Father in heaven, who hears her speak,
    A blessing for every child.

SEA SLUMBER-SONG

By Roden Noel

Sea-birds are asleep,
The world forgets to weep,

Sea murmurs her soft slumber-song
On the shadowy sand
Of this elfin land;
"I, the Mother mild,
Hush thee, O my child,
Forget the voices wild!
Isles in elfin light
Dream, the rocks and caves,
Lull'd by whispering waves,
Veil their marbles bright,
Foam glimmers faintly white
Upon the shelly sand
Of this elfin land;
Sea-sound, like violins,
To slumber woos and wins,
I murmur my soft slumber-song,
Leave woes, and wails, and sins,
Ocean's shadowy might
Breathes good-night,
　　Good-night!"

MOTHER-SONG *

By Alfred Austin

White little hands!
　Pink little feet!
Dimpled all over,
　Sweet, sweet, sweet!
What dost thou wail for?
　The unknown? the unseen?

The ills that are coming,
  The joys that have been?

Cling to me closer,
  Closer and closer,
Till the pain that is purer
  Hath banish'd the grosser.
Drain, drain at the stream, love,
  Thy hunger is freeing,
That was born in a dream, love,
  Along with thy being!

Little fingers that feel
For their home on my breast,
Little lips that appeal
For their nurture, their rest!
Why, why dost thou weep, dear?
  Nay, stifle thy cries,
Till the dew of thy sleep, dear,
  Lies soft on thine eyes.

* By permission of The Macmillan Company.

VIII

STORIES

ON THE OTHER TRAIN. A CLOCK'S STORY

ANONYMOUS

"There, Simmons, you blockhead! Why didn't you trot that old woman aboard her train? She'll have to wait here now until the 1:05 A. M."

"You didn't tell me."

"Yes, I did tell you. 'Twas your confounded stupid carelessness."

"She —

"She! You fool! What else could you expect of her! Probably she hasn't any wit; besides, she isn't bound on a very jolly journey — got a pass up the road to the poorhouse. I'll go and tell her, and if you forget her to-night, see if I don't make mince-meat of you!" and our worthy ticket agent shook his fist menacingly at his subordinate.

"You've missed your train, marm," he remarked, coming forward to a queer-looking bundle in the corner.

A trembling hand raised the faded black veil, and revealed the sweetest old face I ever saw.

"Never mind," said a quivering voice.

"'Tis only three o'clock now; you'll have to wait until the night train, which doesn't go up until 1:05."

" Very well, sir; I can wait."

" Wouldn't you like to go to some hotel? Simmons will show you the way."

" No, thank you, sir. One place is as good as another to me. Besides, I have no money."

" Very well," said the agent, turning away indifferently. " Simmons will tell you when it's time."

All the afternoon she sat there so quiet that I thought she must be asleep, but when I looked more closely I could see every once in a while a great tear rolling down her cheek, which she would wipe away hastily with her colored handkerchief.

The station was crowded, and all was bustle and hurry until the 9:50 train going east came due; then every passenger left but the old lady. It is very rare indeed that any one takes the night express, and almost always after ten o'clock the station becomes silent and empty.

The ticket agent put on his great-coat, and, bidding Simmons keep his wits about him for once in his life, departed for home.

But he had no sooner gone than that functionary stretched himself out upon the table, as usual, and began to snore vociferously.

Then it was that I witnessed such a sight as I never had before and never expect to witness again.

The fire had gone down — it was a cold night and the wind howled dismally outside. The lamps grew dim and flared, casting weird shadows on the wall.

By and by I heard a smothered sob from the corner, then another. I looked in that direction. She had risen from her seat, and oh, the look of agony on that poor pinched face!

"I can't believe it! My babies! my babies! how often have I held them in my arms and kissed them; and how often they used to say back to me, 'I love you, mamma,' and now, O God! they've turned against me! Where am I going? To the poorhouse! No! no! no! I can not! I will not! Oh, the disgrace!"

And sinking on her knees, she sobbed out in prayer: "O God, spare me this and take me home! O God, spare me this disgrace; spare me!"

The wind rose higher and swept through the crevices, icy cold. How it moaned and seemed to sob like something human that is hurt! I began to shake, but the kneeling figure never stirred. The thin shawl had dropped from her shoulders unheeded. Simmons turned over and drew his blanket more closely about him.

Oh, how cold! Only one lamp remained, burning dimly; the other two had gone out for want of oil. I could hardly see, it was so dark.

At last she became quieter and ceased to moan. Then I grew drowsy, and kinder lost run of things after I had struck twelve, when some one entered the station with a bright light. I started up. It was the brightest light I ever saw, and seemed to fill the room full of glory. I could see 'twas a man. He walked to the kneeling figure and touched her upon the shoulder. She started up and turned her face wildly around. I heard him say:

" 'Tis **train**-time, ma'am.　Come!"

" I am ready," she whispered.

" Then give me your pass, ma'am."

She reached him a worn old book, which he took, and from it read aloud:

" Come unto me, all ye that labor and are heavy laden, and I will give you rest."

" That's the pass over our road, ma'am.　Are you ready?"

The light died away, and darkness fell in its place. My hand touched the stroke of one.　Simmons awoke with a start and snatched his lantern.　The whistle sounded " down brakes"; the train was due.　He ran to the corner and shook the old woman.

" Wake up, marm; 'tis train-time."

But she never heeded.　He gave one look at the white, set face, and, dropping his lantern, fled.

The up train halted, the conductor shouted " All aboard," but no one made a move that way.

The next morning, when the ticket agent came, he found her frozen to death.　They whispered among themselves, and the coroner made out the verdict " apoplexy" and it was in some way hushed up.

They laid her out in the station, and advertised for her friends, but no one came.　So, after the second day, they buried her.

The last look on the sweet old face, lit up with a smile so heavenly, I keep with me yet; and when I think of the occurrence of that night, I know she went out on the other train, which never stopped at the poorhouse.

THE CAMP FIRE MOTHER *

By Mrs. L. H. Gulick and Ethel Rogers

When Mary joined the Camp Fire, neither she nor her mother really knew what it meant. Mary wanted to join because all the other girls belonged, and because the girls looked so cute in those Indian dresses. Besides they were going camping next summer and she wanted to go too.

Mother sighed a little and said, " Well, I suppose you may, but it will mean just one thing more to pay for and to dress you for. It does seem as if I never had you at home any more. Still, I don't want you to miss the fun the other girls are having."

So Mary went dancing off to tell the girls she could join before mother had time to change her mind, and then danced back to her practicing. Mary's mother meanwhile went back to the kitchen and to her meditations about how to make her allowance for spring clothes provide the sort of outfit Mary would need. After all, she said to herself, Mary must have her chance. It was all very well for mother to have a life of drudgery, but her daughter was to be fitted for something better. She went to the telephone and explained to a friend that she could not come Friday night, because Mary was going to a party and could not stay with the children. " She's getting to the popular age, you know," she said, with a ring of pride in her voice.

And then, being rather human, she sat down all by

herself and cried because she was losing her little girl.

Other mothers had told her the time would come. But was there no other way?

Then Mary's mother had the surprise of her life. The Camp Fire gave her back her daughter. She was incredulous at first, as who would not have been? For when Mary came home from the Camp Fire meeting, she promptly offered to stay with the children Friday evening. " I've started to earn an honor for taking care of the baby for an hour every day," she said, " and I'll be out late Friday afternoon, so I'll just have to stay at home at night. And say, mother, there's an honor for pressing a suit. Do you suppose you could teach me to do mine this time, instead of doing it for me? You see Frances will get honors fast, because she's staying out of school, and I don't want her to get to be a Wood Gatherer before I do."

This was the beginning. But as the new experience unfolded something not mentioned in the list of honors took place, intangibly but surely, in the lives of Mary and her mother. Acquiring the honors necessitated taking lessons of mother, whose skill in setting a table, baking a loaf of bread or turning out a light cake or a beautiful jar of canned fruit suddenly kindled a new respect in her daughter's mind. The line between drudgery and refined knowledge softened a little. An element of fun crept even into mother's work, as she entered by proxy the thrilling race for honors. Also a more solemn joy, a sense of fellowship in something abiding and beautiful, as she learned to chant with her daughter the Fire-Maker's Desire:

> For I will tend
> As my fathers have tended
> And my father's fathers since time began
> The fire that is called
> The love of man for man
> The love of man for God.

The knowledge that her mother had given her the secret of the creative activities that had their center in the hearthfire and the home, seemed to her suddenly a sacred treasure which must be handed down undiminished through her daughter's hands to the long line of womanhood to come. . . .

The story of Mary and her mother is not a myth, neither is it an exceptional case. It is typical of the thing that is happening in the thousands of homes into which Camp Fire has made its way. . . .

A mother tells how wistfully she had longed to have a greater share in her daughter's growth, but it had seemed impossible when the school demanded so much of her time and her interests were all outside the home. " Now she is so interested in everything in the home," she said, " and calls on me to help her solve such knotty problems as how to clean the ice chest or how to care for hardwood floors. She is studying baby brother so intently that I believe she knows better than I do what he wants when he cries."

One might think this would satisfy the average Guardian, to know that the mother's influence is back of her every effort, helping the daughter to be faithful in her attendance at meetings and giving her instruction and encouragement in winning her honors. But the part of the Camp Fire mother has in many places become larger and more definite than this. Mothers are giving lessons to the Camp Fire as a whole in the special forms of handcraft or homecraft in which they happen to excel. Of course the ambition of the Camp Fire girl is to learn not only to do the things but to do them by the best modern methods. The mother who has studied scientifically the problem of marketing has something too valuable to be ignored in the training of the group. The one who is an expert seamstress or who delights in fine laundering can give the girls a profitable forenoon, if not a whole series of lessons in her specialty. . . .

Camp Fire is bringing to mothers the vision that romance and beauty are not dead in themselves, and that except as they themselves can live joyously, entering into life with the enthusiasm of youth, they can not either understand or be understood by their children.

This situation is bringing about a discovery — that the capacity for these things has not died out during the years; it has only been repressed and now it bursts forth afresh, the enthusiasm of youth backed by the strength of mature experience. This is the kind of leadership the children long for and love. This they understand. And through this they are shaped in character and ideals, shaped not by the forces of external compulsion but by those of deepest desire. The

Camp Fire mother is venturing into unknown deeps, and reveling in her act with something of the shy, pleased, free feeling of the mother who takes off her shoes and stockings, and goes wading with the children in the brook, enjoying it every bit as much as the children themselves. . . .

One Guardian has written, " I want you to know that in one instance at least your Camp Fire has done as much for the Guardian as for the girls. You have given her a purpose in life, and seventeen dear daughters to mitigate the ever-present loss of the little girl who left me. I never would have known one of them if it were not for the beautiful Camp Fire idea."

Do you see? There is a great deal of pent-up motherhood in the world, motherhood that has been denied its natural expression, or that is large enough to reach out to more than its own small brood, if the chance were given. Girls that have lost their mothers, girls that never had any in the real sense, girls whose mothers are too burdened to give them all the mothering they need — we have them always with us. The Camp Fire brings the mother-love and hungry heart together. Itself a mother's conception, wrought out while striving to give her own daughters the preparation for womanhood that she wished them to have, Camp Fire is the expression of the Mother Spirit brooding over society and the world.

* *By permission of " Wohelo," Camp Fire Girls, inc.*

NOT TOO LATE

By Katharine McDowell Rice

" Why do I act so, I wonder? " Agatha frankly asked herself. " I'm just as cross as I can be. Marion, come back," she called. " Come back and I'll do it."

But the little feet in the unbuttoned shoes had pattered far away.

" I believe I'm ill-natured toward everybody in the house," said Agatha as she went back to her seat by the window. " I really believe I am. Why, actually," she acknowledged a moment later, and her cheeks began to burn, " I have been impatient with everybody in the family, and just since I've come in from school ! "

Agatha rapidly reviewed the last two hours. Her mother had asked her to find a piece of twine in the string-bag, and Agatha had answered, " Oh, I do hate to go to that old string-bag; the things always come tumbling out ! " And her mother had said " Agatha ! " in a reproachful tone, the remembrance of which was making Agatha say to herself now, " I wish mamma wouldn't say ' Agatha ' to me that way. I always think of it after I get to bed, and it makes me feel bad.

" Why, I was cross to mamma even before that," she went on with almost a start, " when I snatched my letter from her and said she needn't have opened it. And then after lunch when mamma asked me if I didn't want to hear Aunt Fanny read some poetry, I said, ' I don't care for poetry,' and mamma said, ' I think you must be tired, dear.' Mamma is always thinking I must be tired when I act that way, but I wasn't tired; I was just ill-tempered. I'm a cross-patch; that's what I am. Dick said I was when I took my paints away from him — and I am."

She had gotten up and was looking out of the window. Down on the sidewalk Marion was dancing along at Judith's side. She had her doll with her and was evidently going to the park. Agatha knocked on the window, but they did not hear her.

" Isn't she just the sweetest little thing in the world!" said Agatha with a growing lump in her throat as she watched the tiny shoes that somebody had buttoned carry the small sister out of sight. " And to think I told her she was big enough to button her own shoes, and that she ought to be ashamed to come to me!"

Agatha went down to the library. Mamma smiled a welcome, and motioned to a seat at her side.

"Wait a moment, will you, please, Fanny?" said mamma. " I want to explain to Agatha that these verses were written by a man named William Cowper, who was looking at his mother's portrait as he wrote them."

Then Aunt Fanny went on with the poem where she had stopped when Agatha came in,—

> May I but meet thee on that peaceful shore,

and Agatha listened to all that followed with intense interest.

When the poem was finished, and all were saying how beautiful it was, and thanking Aunt Fanny for reading it, Agatha said:

"And did his mother come back to him?"

"Come back to him!" echoed Aunt Clara. "Why, didn't you understand, child, that his mother was dead?"

"Dead!" cried Agatha. "Why, he spoke of her going away somewhere — somewhere in a ship. Oh, mamma! she was not dead?" And she turned beseechingly to her mother.

"Yes, dear," said mamma, putting an arm tenderly about her little daughter, for Agatha was crying.

"A child is too emotional to hear such things," said Aunt Clara. "We should have read something lighter after Agatha came in."

"Oh, no," said Agatha, looking up through her tears. "I think it was beautiful, Aunt Clara. But are you all sure that she was dead?"

"Yes. See here, Agatha;" and Aunt Fanny read aloud, pointing to the line as she did so,—

My mother, when I learned that thou wast dead,

and Agatha's eyes followed the words.

"That part was all read before Agatha came in — I remember it now," said her mother.

"I never knew anything so sad," said the little girl earnestly,— so earnestly that the aunts smiled at each other, and Aunt Clara motioned to Aunt Fanny to put away the book.

"Oh, don't put it away!" pleaded Agatha, "please don't. I should like to read it myself."

"You cannot understand it, child," said Aunt Clara. "It wasn't written for young girls."

"But I'm so sorry for him!" said Agatha, "for you say it's all true. Sometimes, you know, people who write poetry only imagine things, Aunt Clara. Wouldn't it have been beautiful if after the son had written it all, his mother had been alive and had come back! Then he would have known how dreadfully he felt when he thought she was dead, and he would always have been so kind and lovely to her afterwards."

"I think children are too imaginative to hear these things," said Aunt Clara. "It is bad for them. Time enough to think of such things when they get older."

"Oh, they forget them straightway," said Aunt Fanny.

But Agatha did not forget. She begged to hear the poem again that night before she went to bed, and her mother read it, explaining all that Agatha did not fully understand. And when it was finished, she said in a broken voice, her arms about her mother's neck:

"I am so glad I can look at your picture, mamma, and know that your lips can still speak! And I mean to be a great deal better to you, and better to Dick and to Marion and everybody. I've asked God to help me. And oh, I'm so glad I've heard the poem in time!"

NIOBE

By Thomas Bulfinch

The fate of Arachne was noised abroad through all the country, and served as a warning to all presumptuous mortals not to compare themselves with the divinities. But one, and she a matron too, failed to learn the lesson of humility. It was Niobe, the queen of Thebes. She had indeed much to be proud of; but it was not her husband's fame, nor her own beauty, nor their great descent, nor the power of their kingdom that elated her. It was her children; and truly the happiest of mothers would Niobe have been, if only she had not claimed to be so. It was on occasion of the annual celebration in honor of Latona and her offspring, Apollo and Diana, when the people of Thebes were assembled, their brows crowned with laurel, bearing frankincense to the altars and paying their vows,— that Niobe appeared among the crowd. Her attire was splendid with gold and gems, and her aspect beautiful as the face of an angry woman can be. She stood and surveyed the people with haughty looks. "What folly," said she, "is this!— to prefer beings whom you never saw to those who stand before your eyes! Why should Latona be honored with worship, and none paid to me? My father was Tantalus, who was received as a guest at the table of the gods; my mother was a goddess. My husband built and rules this city, Thebes, and Phrygia is my paternal inheritance. Wherever I turn my eyes I survey the elements of my power; nor is my form and presence unworthy of a goddess. To all this let me add, I have seven sons and seven daughters, and look for sons-in-law and daughters-in-law of pretensions worthy of my alliance. Have I not cause for pride? Will you prefer to me this Latona, the Titan's daughter, with her two children? I have seven times as many. Fortunate indeed am I, and fortunate I shall remain! Will any one deny this? My abundance is my security. I feel myself too strong for Fortune to subdue. She may take from me much; I shall still have much left. Were I to lose some of my children, I should hardly be left as poor as Latona with her two only. Away with you from these solemnities,— put off the laurel from your brows,— have done with this worship!" The people obeyed, and left the sacred services uncompleted.

The goddess was indignant. On the Cynthian mountain top, where she dwelt, she thus addressed her son and daughter: "My children, I who have been so proud of you both, and have been used to hold myself second to none of the goddesses except Juno alone, begin now to doubt whether I am indeed a goddess. I shall be deprived of my worship altogether unless you protect me." She was proceeding in this strain, but Apollo interrupted her. "Say no more," said he; "speech only delays punishment." So said Diana also. Darting through the air, veiled in clouds, they alighted on the towers of the city. Spread out before the gates was a broad plain, where the youth of the city pursued their war-like sports.

The sons of Niobe were there with the rest,— some mounted on spirited horses richly caparisoned, some driving gay chariots. Ismenos, the first-born, as he guided his foaming steeds, struck with an arrow from above, cried out, " Ah, me! "— dropped the reins and fell lifeless. Another hearing the sound of the bow, — like a boatman who sees the storm gathering and makes all sail for port,— gave the rein to his horses and attempted to escape. The inevitable arrow overtook him as he fled. Two others, younger boys, just from their tasks, had gone to the play-ground to have a game of wrestling. As they stood breast to breast, one arrow pierced them both. They uttered a cry together, together cast a parting look around them, and together breathed their last. Alphenor, an elder brother, seeing them fall, hastened to the spot to render assistance, and fell stricken in the act of brotherly duty. One only was left, Ilioneus. He raised his arms to heaven to try whether prayer might not avail. " Spare me, ye gods! " he cried, addressing all, in his ignorance that all needed not his intercessions; and Apollo would have spared him, but the arrow had already left the string and it was too late.

The terror of the people and grief of the attendants soon made Niobe acquainted with what had taken place. She could hardly think it possible; she was indignant that the gods had dared and amazed that they had been able to do it. Her husband, Amphion, overwhelmed with the blow, destroyed himself. Alas! how different was this Niobe from her who had so lately driven away the people from the sacred rites,

and held her stately course through the city, the envy
of her friends, now the pity even of her foes! She
knelt over the lifeless bodies, and kissed, now one,
now another of her dead sons. Raising her pallid
arms to heaven, "Cruel Latona," said she, "feed full
your rage with my anguish! Satiate your hard heart,
while I follow to the grave my seven sons. Yet where
is your triumph? Bereaved as I am, I am still richer
than you, my conqueror." Scarce had she spoken,
when the bow sounded and struck terror into all hearts
except Niobe's alone. She was brave from excess of
grief. The sisters stood in garments of mourning
over the biers of their dead brothers. One fell,
struck by an arrow, and died on the corpse she was
bewailing. Another, attempting to console her
mother, suddenly ceased to speak, and sank lifeless
to the earth. A third tried to escape by flight, a fourth
by concealment, another stood trembling, uncertain
what course to take. Six were now dead, and only
one remained, whom the mother held clasped in her
arms, and covered as it were with her whole body.
" Spare me one, and that the youngest! O, spare me
one of so many!" she cried; and while she spoke,
that one fell dead. Desolate she sat, among sons,
daughters, husband, all dead, and seemed torpid with
grief. The breeze moved not her hair, no color was
on her cheek, her eyes glared fixed and immovable,
there was no sign of life about her.

Her very tongue cleaved to the roof of her mouth,
and her veins ceased to convey the tide of life. Her
neck bent not, her arms made no gesture, her foot

no step. She was changed to stone, within and without. Yet tears continued to flow; and, borne on a whirlwind to her native mountain, she still remains, a mass of rock, from which a trickling stream flows, the tribute of her never-ending grief.

HAPPY ENDING IN REAL LIFE

By Otto McFeely.

Mr. McFeely tells a story of reality. It is realism that shows the way out of one of the jungles of life and reports the first act in what appears to be the greatest reform since the public school took the place of the charity school.

In the first week of June, 1911, a woman with three children, two clinging to her skirts and one snuggling in her lap, sat in a straight-back chair before a judge in the juvenile court of Chicago. This court room was across the street from Hull house, and a block from the Mary Crane Day nursery. A dozen agents of organized charity were there to aid in solving the problem of the destitute mother. A probation officer reported on the " case." The destitute mother, in court terminology, is a " case."

Mrs. Brian * was a typical " case." Eight months before her husband had been injured while at work in the steel mills. He lived a few weeks and then died. The woman had gone through the grade and high schools and had hope of a decent life. When

* The identity of this mother is concealed under a fictitious name.

the accident occurred they had $500 saved up, and were about to buy a home on the installment plan.

The doctors and living expenses, before the workman died, took part of this hoard, so painfully gathered. After the funeral Mrs. Brian set out to earn a living for herself and her three children, the oldest under five years, and one an infant. Like thousands of other women, she thought of keeping roomers, and used the last of her savings to pay an installment on a furnished house in the poor district, where she expected to shelter homeless working people at so much per week.

The business failed, as it was destined to do. A woman with three children cannot keep up a rooming house even for poorly paid working people. One after another of the guests left, and this bright day in June found her in the dingy juvenile court, where she had been taken by agents of organized charity.

One of these agents reported: " Your Honor, this woman is about to be set out on the street. She can not pay her rent. But she is able to work and we plan to place her children in an institution, so she can go to work somewhere."

" I don't know what to do," said the mother to the judge. " This lady said, when I asked her for help, that I would have to ' put my children away ' and go to work. I wish there was some other way," and she held her baby closer and tried to include the two standing at her knee in the protecting embrace.

" Did you collect anything from the steel company? " asked the judge.

"Not yet; my case comes up in about three months," she said, hopefully, but the distracted face of the judge did not reflect that hope. He knew the courts and the steel business too well.

He had been on that bench for three years. Almost daily he held conference with the world's most famous charity workers. All Protestant and Catholic churches of the great city had paid agents there to help. Thousands were raised by charity, ostensibly to relieve just such persons as Mrs. Brian.

The judge, probation officers and charity agents held a little conference.

"Where shall we send the children?" was the question.

They knew no other way. Not one of these court officers, nor charity experts, could conceive of any other way than to break up the family — taking these children away from their mother, the supreme crime of civilization, punishment worse than death for the offense of poverty.

For three years the judge had seen this thing go on. His face was haggard, he looked as if he was ready for the hospital. He was too humane to do this awful thing day after day and not to feel it. The charity workers appeared to be less affected.

To send the babies to an institution would cost the county $10 a month for each child — $30 in all. They were ready to pay this sum to an asylum for taking care of these poverty-stricken children, but there was no way the money could be paid to the mother for performing the functions for which nature intended her, and for which she was so well prepared.

The ax was about to fall. The wagon was backed up at the door. Trim nurses entered to take the babies from their mother's arms, in all probability forever, when something happened.

During the progress of the " trial " two men entered. One of them was Judge Henry Neil, who for a year had been watching this destruction of families — the punishment of women and children for poverty, and all in the name of " kindness."

That very week Governor Deneen had signed a bill that was to revolutionize the practice of the juvenile court and to prevent the separation of mothers and their children in the name of sweet charity — a habit that had become so common that it was then a vested right of the charity organizations.

Neil had presented the bill to the legislature, and it was such a little thing that it crept through almost unnoticed. Organized charity experts knew nothing of it. It was an amendment to the juvenile court act in these words:

" If the parent or parents of such dependent or neglected child are poor and unable to properly care for said child, but are otherwise proper guardians, and it is for the welfare of such child to remain at home, the court may enter an order finding such facts and fixing the amount of money necessary to enable the parent or parents to properly care for such child, and thereupon it shall be the duty of the county board, through its county agent, or otherwise, to pay to such parent or parents, at such times as said order may designate, the amount so specified for the care of such dependent or neglected child until the further order of the court."

This law was to go into force July 1, 1911. The Brian family was to be broken up, nevertheless, because poverty can not wait three weeks. Neil conferred with the judge. He agreed to pay Mrs. Brian $25 a month until the pension law went into effect, and on July 1, the very day the act became useful, Mrs. Brian was pensioned, the first woman who ever drew a pension for being a mother. She still lives with her own children, and since then almost 2,000 mothers have been pensioned in Chicago alone, and the system to-day is at work from the Atlantic to the Pacific.

THE MOTHER

BY ROBERT HAVEN SCHAUFFLER

All day her watch had lasted on the plateau above the town. And now the sun slanted low over the dull, blue sheen of the western sea, playing changingly with the angular mountain which rose abruptly from its surge.

The young matron did not heed the magic which was transforming the theater of hills to the north and lingering lovingly at last on the eastern summit. Nor had she any eyes for the changing hue of the ivy-clad cubes of stone that formed the village over which her hungry gaze passed, sweeping the length and breadth of the plain below.

She seemed not much above thirty: tall, erect, and lithe. Her throat, bared to the breeze, was of the purest modeling; her skin of a whiteness unusual in that warm climate. Her head, a little small for her rounded figure, was crowned with a coil of chestnut hair, and her eyes glowed with a look strange to the common light of every day. It was her soul that was scanning that southward country.

From time to time she would fondle a small object hidden beneath the white folds of her robe. Once she threw her arms out in a passionate gesture toward the plain, and tears overflowed the beautiful eyes. Again she fell on her knees, and the throes of inner prayer found relief at her lips:

"Father, my Father, grant me to see him ere the dusk!"

Once again she sank down, moaning:

"He is in Thine everlasting arms. But Thou, who knowest times and seasons, give him to me on this day of days!"

Under the curve of a shielding hand her vision strained through the clear, pure air,— strained and found at last two specks far out in the plain, and followed them breathlessly as they crept nearer. One traveler was clad in a dark garment, and stopped presently, leaving his light-robed companion to hasten on alone toward the hungry-eyed woman on the plateau.

All at once she gathered her skirt with a joyous cry and ran down through the village.

They met on a low, rounded hill near the plain.

"My son, my darling!" she cried, catching him

passionately to her bosom. " We have searched, and waited, and agonized," she continued after a pause, smiling at him through her happy tears. " But it matters nothing now. I have thee again."

" My mother," said the boy as he caressed her cheek, looking at her dreamily, " I have been with my cousin. Even now he waits below for me. I must bid thee farewell. I must pass from thy face forever."

His lip trembled a little, but he smiled bravely. " For it is the will of God, the Father."

The mother's face went ashen. She tottered and would have fallen but for his slender arm about her.

Her thoughts were whirling in wild confusion, yet she knew that she must decide calmly, wisely, quickly.

Her lips moved, but made no sound.

" Oh, lay Thy wise and gracious hand upon me ! " was what she breathed in silence.

Then her voice sounded rich and happy and fresh, as it had always sounded for him.

" His will be done. Thou comest to bid farewell to thy brothers and father ? "

" It may not be," he answered. " My lot henceforth is to flee the touch of the world, the unsympathetic eye, the ribald tongue of those like my brothers — the defilement of common life."

The mother pressed him closer.

" Say all that is in thine heart," she murmured. " We will bide here."

They sank down together on the soft, bright turf,

facing the brilliance of the west, she holding her child as of old in the hollow of her arm.

He began to speak.

"For long and long a voice within me said, 'Go and seek thy cousin.' So I sought and found, and we abode together in the woods and fields, and were friends with our dear brothers the beasts, and the fishes, and the birds. There, day by day, my cousin would tell me of the dream that filled his soul and of the holy men who had put the dream there."

The mother's eyes grew larger with a swift terror, but she held her peace.

"And at the last, when the beauty, the wind, the sun, the rain, and the voice of God, had purified me in some measure, my cousin brought me to visit these holy men."

The clear, boyish voice rose and began to vibrate with enthusiasm.

"Ah, mother, *they* are the chosen ones of God! Sweet and grave and gentle they are, and theirs is the perfect life. They dwell spotless and apart from the world. They own one common purse, and spend their lives working with their hands and pondering and dreaming on purity, goodness, and the commands of the great law."

He sprang up in his excitement and stood erect and wide-eyed before her.

"Ah, mother, they are so good that they would do nothing on the Sabbath, even to saving their own lives or the lives of their animals, or their brothers.

They bathe very often in sacred water. They have no wives, and mortify the flesh, and ——"

"What is their aim in this?" the mother interrupted gently.

The boy was aflame with his subject.

"Ah, that is it — the great goal toward which they all run," he cried. "They are doing my Father's work, and I must help! Hear, hear what is before me: When a young novice comes to them they give him the symbols of purity: a spade, an apron, and a white robe to wear at the holy meals. In a year he receives a closer fellowship and the baths of purification. After that he enters the state of bodily purity. Then little by little he enters into purity of the spirit, meekness, holiness. He becomes a temple of the Holy Spirit, and prophesies. Ah, think, mother, how sweet it would be to lie entranced there for days and weeks in an earthly paradise, with no rough world to break the spell, while the angels sing softly in one's ears! I, even I, have already tasted of that bliss."

"Say on," she breathed. "What does the holy man do then?"

"Then," the inspired, boyish tones continued — "then he performs miracles, and finally —" he clasped her hand convulsively —"he becomes Elias, the forerunner of the Messiah!"

From far out in the wilderness came a melancholy cry.

"It is John, my cousin," said the boy, radiant, half turning himself at the sound. "I must go to him."

She drew in her breath sharply, and rose.

" Bear a message to John," she said. " Not pour-
ings of water, nor white robes; not times and seasons,
nor feasts in darkness and silence, shall hasten the
kingdom of heaven; neither formulas, nor phylacter-
ies, nor madness on the Sabbath. Above all, no self-
ish, proud isolation shall usher in the glorious reign
of the Messiah. These holy men,— these Essenes,—
are but stricter, sterner, nobler Pharisees. Tell thy
cousin to take all the noble and fine, to reject all the
selfish and unmeaning, in their lives. Doctrine is not
in heaven. Not by fasts and scourgings, not by vigils
and scruples about the law; not by selfishly shutting
out the world, but by taking all poor, suffering, erring,
striving humanity into his heart will he become the
true Elias."

There was a breathless, thrilling moment of perfect
silence as the glowing eyes of the mother looked deep
into the astonished, questioning eyes of the son.

Then she rested both hands on his shoulders and
spoke almost in a whisper.

" As for thee, the time is now come. Does my son
know what this day means? "

He looked at her wonderingly and was silent.

The mother spoke:

" For many years I have kept these things and
pondered them in my heart. Now, *now* the hour is
here when thou must know them."

She bent so close that a strand of loosened hair
swept his forehead.

" In the time before thou wert born came as in
a dream a wondrous visitor to me straight from the

Father. And that pure, ecstatic messenger announced that the power of the Highest would overshadow me, and that my child was to be the son of the Highest, who should save His people from their sins — the Prince of Peace — the Messiah!"

From the wilderness came a long, melancholy cry, but the rapt boy heard not.

The mother continued in the soft, tender voice that began to tremble.

"This day is thy birthday. Twelve years ago this eventide, when thou camest into the world of men, men came to worship and praise God for thee,— the lowliest and the highest,— as a token that thou wert to be not only Son of God but Son of Man as well. Poor, ignorant shepherds crowded about us in that little stable where we lay, and left the sweet savor of their prayers, and tears, and rejoicings. And great, wise kings from another part of the earth came also."

From beneath the folds of her robe she drew forth by a fine-spun chain an intricately chased casket of soft, yellow gold.

The boy took it dreamily into his hands, and as his fingers opened it, there floated forth upon the air of the hills of Nazareth the sacred odor of incense mingled with a perfume indescribably delicate and precious.

"Read!" whispered the mother.

The boy held his breath suddenly.

There, on the lower surface of the lid, graven in

rude characters, as if on the inspiration of the moment, stood the single word

LOVE

She flung wide her arms as if to embrace the universe.

"Love! Love! Love!" she cried in her rich mother's voice. "It is the greatest thing in the world! It is the message of the Messiah!"

The heavens over the sea were of molten gold, and a golden glow seemed to radiate from the boyish face that confronted them. In their trance-like ecstasy the wonderful eyes gazed full into the blinding west — gazed on and on until day had passed into night.

One iterant sound alone, as it drew closer, stirred the silence of that evening: it was the voice of one crying in the wilderness.

IX

PROGRAMS

PROGRAMS

No. I

Proclamation for Mothers' Day, of President or Governor.

Song — By the School.

Reading — Selection: —" Mother Love," by Albert Barnes.

Solo —" Mother o' Mine " (Music by Tours).

Reading — Selection: —" Niobe," by Frederick Tennyson.

Recitation.

Song —" The White Carnation."

(Tune: " Ten Thousand Times Ten Thousand ")

> Oh, white carnation chosen
>   For purity, for light,
> For sweetness, for endurance
>   Of love beyond our sight!
>
> Oh, white carnation blessed
>   When worn on loyal breast
> Of son or daughter, telling
>   Of love the highest, best!

Selections.

For School Exercises the Friday Before Mothers' Day

No. II

Proclamation for Mothers' Day, of President or Governor.

Song —" The White Carnation."

A Short Address on Mothers' Day by the Principal.

A Play by the Dramatic Club: —" Demeter — A Mask."

" Dreams and the Light Imaginings of Men "
By Robert Bridges.

Written for the ladies of Somerville College and acted by them at the inauguration of their new building in 1904.

For Church Service

Hymn —" Blest Be the Tie That Binds."

Prayer.

Mothers' Day Proclamation.

Scripture Reading — Proverbs xxxi, 10–31

Solo — The Magnificat (Canticle 37)

Scripture Reading — Hannah's Song of Thanksgiving.

Offertory — For " Little Mothers."

Sermon.

Song —" The White Carnation."

Collection of Flowers *

* It is requested that all bring bunches of white flowers, these to be collected after the sermon by a few young girls of the Church, who will lay them in a great mound in front of the Altar. These are later to be taken to old ladies' homes and hospitals in the city, or if in the country, to mothers' graves or to the sick.

Hymn —" For all the Saints a Noble Throng."
Benediction.

For Sunday School

Hymn —" By Cool Siloam's Shady Rill."
Short Prayer — By Superintendent.
The Lord's Prayer — In Unison.
Scripture Reading — I. Samuel, iii 1–21.
Hymn or Solo —" Hushed was the Evening Hymn."
Recitations — By the Children of the School.
Selection from Scripture — St. John xix 26–27.
Litany (Solo) The Words on the Cross, Part III
" Jesu, loving to the end."
Address — Text St. John xix 26–27.
Offertory — For Fresh Air Fund.
Hymn —" When all Thy Mercies, O my God."
Collection of Flowers * (for Mothers' Graves).
Prayer — For Mothers.
Benediction — By the Pastor.

* All having been requested to wear or carry flowers (the flower worn should be the white carnation), these will be collected by four little girls and boys carrying baskets which will be laid in front of the pulpit.